MILITARY VEHICLES

568

MILITARY VEHICLES

FROM WORLD WAR I TO THE PRESENT

HANS HALBERSTADT

MetroBooks

MetroBooks
An Imprint of Friedman/Fairfax Publishers

© 1998 by Michael Friedman Publishing Group, Inc.

All rights reserved. No part of this publication may be reproduced, stored in a retrieval system, or transmitted, in any form or by any means, electronic, mechanical, photocopying, recording, or otherwise, without prior written permission from the publisher.

Library of Congress Cataloging-in-Publication Data

Halberstadt, Hans.
Military Vehicles: World War I to the Present / by Hans Halberstadt.
p. cm.
Includes index.
ISBN 1-56799-594-2
1. Vehicles, Military–United States–History–20th Century.
I. Title.
UG618.H35 1998
623.7' 47–dc21 98-6296

Editor: Ann Kirby
Art Director: Kevin Ullrich
Designer: Galen Smith
Photography Editor: Christopher C. Bain
Production Manager: Jeanne E. Hutter

Color separations by Bright Arts Graphics (S) Pte Ltd.
Printed in Singapore by Tien Wah Press (Pte) Limited
1 3 5 7 9 10 8 6 4 2

For bulk purchases and special sales, please contact:

Friedman/Fairfax Publishers
Attention: Sales Department
15 West 26th Street
New York, NY 10010
212/685-6610 FAX 212/685-1307

Visit our website:
http://www.metrobooks.com

STOCK PHOTOGRAPHY

Most photographs in this book (and about sixty thousand other military stock photos) are available as stock images for editorial and advertising applications. Direct inquiries to:

Military Stock Photos, 240 South 13th Street, San Jose, California 95112 USA phone: (408) 293-8131 fax: (408) 293-8156

DEDICATION

This one is for our own, sweet Kate—Miss Katherine Hope Ensor—a girl with power to spare, great fit and finish, and a *very* independent suspension.

ACKNOWLEDGMENTS

One of the delightful parts of my work as an author of books about military subjects and communities is the generous, cooperative assistance I get from others in this small, specialized brotherhood. When I started writing these books, fifteen years and about forty titles ago, I expected other authors to be aloof and reserved, careful and competitive. Then George Hall, the great aviation and fire-fighting writer and photographer, took me under his wing and gave me some very valuable pointers and contacts. Out in the field I met others, like *Soldiers* magazine's Dennis Steele, and quickly discovered that most military authors and many military journalists are happy to share sources and resources. That has certainly been true on this project. So I am pleased to tip my Helmet, Combat Vehicle Crewman, to:

Mike Green, armor specialist and author of many books on military and law enforcement; Mike was kind enough to share a truckload of references, a whole library's worth, and hundreds of archival and contemporary photographs.

Maj. Will Fowler, ex-British Army public affairs officer and military author and journalist; Will helped immeasurably with the British armor and vehicles, generously sharing references and photography.

Another salute is due Jacques Littlefield, who privately maintains one of the foremost collections of armor in the world, and very generously made much of it available for this book.

I'm also indebted to many members of the Military Vehicle Trust and Military Vehicle Preservation Association. Foremost among the latter is the president of my local branch, Kurt Lesser; my neighbor and friend Joe Cardoza, owner of an excellent Scorpion; and Bren Carrier, who helped with photography and research.

SSG Michael Ellithorp provided excellent information on correct painting and marking of U.S. Army vehicles, plus referrals to Gulf War vets.

Samuel Katz, prolific author and good friend, furnished lots of information and photography on Merkeva and other Israeli systems.

Rick Lathrop provided excellent information about the WC52 and M37 series trucks, and maintains a great website for both, the Unofficial M37 Page.

Andreas Mehlhorn of Braunschweig, Germany, provided most of the data about the fascinating World War II motorcycle half-track called the Kettenkrad.

George R. Bradford, publisher of the fascinating Canadian enthusiast magazine called *AFV News*, supplied lots of excellent contacts, advice, archival material, and his superb line drawings.

SPECIFICATIONS AND VEHICLE DATA

The data on individual vehicles presented in this book may vary from published data in other works. As a rule, I have tried to include information on at least one representative model of each type of vehicle. However, in cases where vehicle models varied widely, I chose not to include such details. The original sources are typically *Jane's* comprehensive reference works; *Tanks and Fighting Vehicles*, by Christopher Foss, published by Chartwell Books; and official manuals where available.

C O N T E N T S

FOREWORD

It is impossible to include in a book of this size all of the thousands of fascinating and important military vehicles in service during this century, or even this decade–it is just too big a topic. I have, therefore, been selective.

Some readers may object to my selections. I have been guided pretty much by my own interests and prejudices, plus the advice and counsel of military vehicle collector friends–not all of which I accepted. I have also relied somewhat on my own experience, both in the U.S. Army and as a longtime student of its systems and soldiers. That experience has included a lot of time in the field, at the National Training Center (NTC) at Fort Irwin, California, where armored units refine their art; at Twentynine Palms, California, where the U.S. Marines do the same thing; and even at the armor center at Kubinka, Russia, where the Russian Army maintains an excellent museum and test center. I have had the rare privilege, for a civilian, to spend extended periods in the field with armor units, ride into "battle" with them at NTC, and learn to fire the main and secondary weapons on the M1 Abrams. All these experiences shaped my choices.

Additionally, this book has been enhanced by the very generous support of Jacques Littlefield, one of the top two private armor collectors in the world. When I had a question about a Matilda, T-34, M5A1 Stuart from World War II, M551 Sheridan from the 1970s, or even the currently popular T-72, it was a simple matter to drive over to Jacques' place, hop in one, and see for myself how the thing was set up. This is valuable in surprising ways: nobody tells you how cramped the Fox turret is, for example, or that the crew of that vehicle has a small built-in oven to warm their rations and tea. You learn things like that from climbing aboard and looking around.

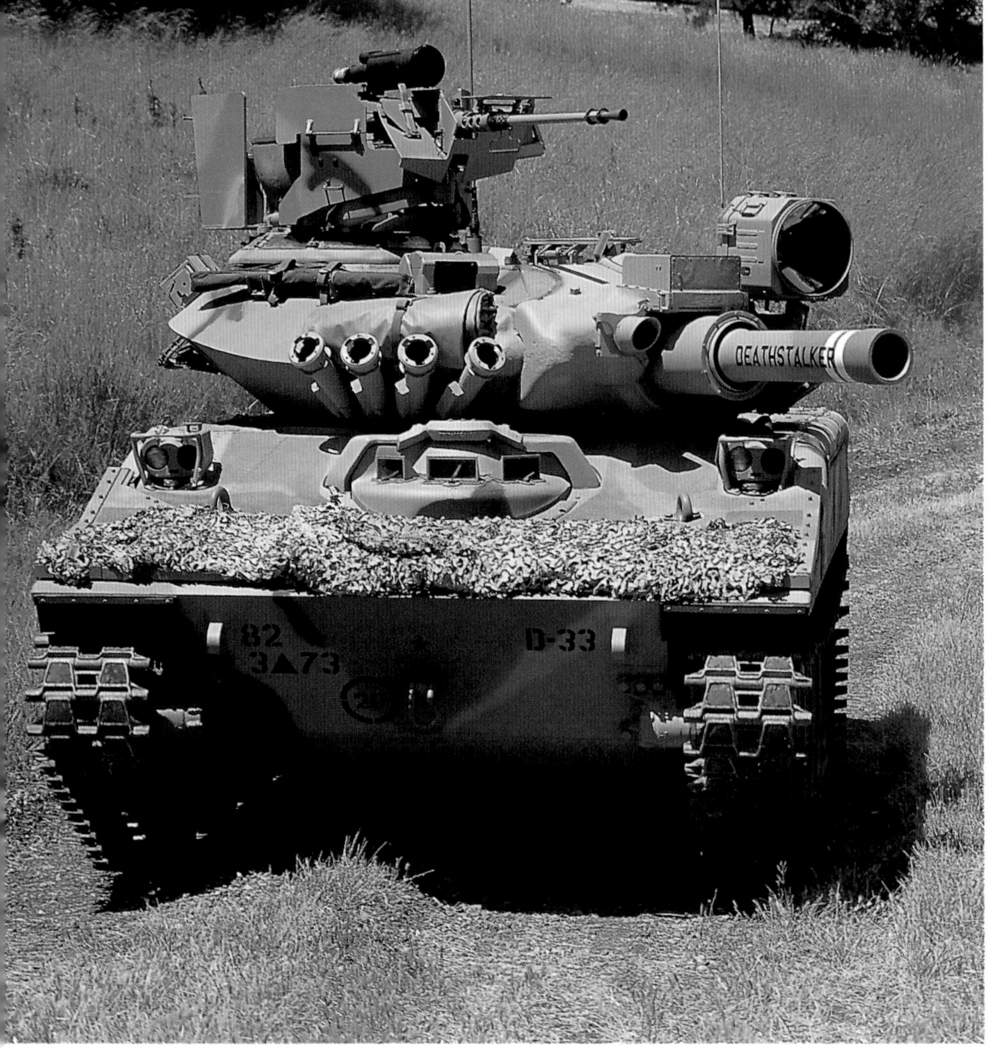

LEFT: M551 Sheridan, recently retired from the 82nd Airborne Division and now in a private collection. OPPOSITE: A Saladin armored car of the 17th/21st Lancers on exercise sometime during the 1950s.

07 BB 21

INTRODUCTION

Mechanization came to the world's military forces about the same time it first came to civilians: experimentally during the very first few years of the twentieth century, then with growing enthusiasm during the years leading up to World War I.

The gasoline-fueled four-stroke cycle engine was developed in the 1880s, perfected sufficiently for practical stationary use over the next twenty years, and then miniaturized and installed in buggies and buckboards. By 1900, cars were becoming commonplace on city streets. Quite suddenly, about 1910, Europeans and Americans developed a raging mania for automobiles and trucks, and a booming market for this new, modern vehicle took off. Trucks of all sizes and capacities, motorbikes and motorcycles, touring cars and tiny buggies appeared on streets and roads all over the world. Some were powered by electricity or steam (both of which worked remarkably well), although gasoline and internal combustion engines dominated. It was a fizzy moment in history, and the world was enthralled.

Professional soldiers way back then were hardly immune to this enthusiasm. Soon enough—1903 for the British Army—the puttering and backfiring of experimental armored cars, little military courier motorbikes, and first-generation trucks were scaring the horses and provoking imaginative profanity from the old troopers. Still, by the start of World War I, motor transport was becoming an accepted part of military operations. It was during that war the first tanks made their fearsome debut.

Trucks were tremendously successful during the war, the tanks less so. Both were obviously the wave of the future, however, and the only real question was how they would be improved.

After the war, very little research and development was done by any of

the nations, at least during the 1920s. While it was obvious that trucks and motorcycles had a place in land warfare, it wasn't so clear what kind of tanks would be needed. Besides, the British, Canadian, American, and French armies had all been bled white of manpower and financial support. All were cut back to skeletal forces on shoestring budgets.

In Germany things were different–worse, in fact. At first, there was barely an army, and less of a budget for one. The German population starved in 1919 and 1920, the poverty due to the disastrous conditions for peace imposed by the victorious Allies. The country, however, proved to be a quick healer.

By 1930 Germany had largely recovered. Even during the dark days of worldwide depression, it managed to rebuild a modern army with modern weapons, vehicles, aircraft, and tactics. When Germany attacked Poland in September 1939, it shocked the world with a new kind of mechanized warfare–fast, coordinated, with an expanded use of trucks, tanks, and motorcycles.

OPPOSITE: Well, it seemed like a good idea at the time–adding simple crawler tracks to an automobile to provide enhanced mobility on soft ground–but it was back to the drawing board soon after this test.

ABOVE: The little Renault FT 17 was one of the very few successful tanks of the formative World War I years. In various forms it served the United States and other nations for many years.

In the sixty years since, the world's military forces have come to depend on all kinds of wheeled transport and fighting vehicles: tanks in many sizes and shapes, armored personnel carriers, mobile rocket and missile launchers, huge supply trucks, and motorcycles for scouts to prowl the edges of the battlefield. There are today massive recovery vehicles that can pull a 60-ton (54.4t) tank out of a shell hole, mobile radar systems to track planes overhead, and specialized combat bulldozers for the engineers. Just as automobiles replaced the horse-drawn carriage in this civilian world, this military mechanization rendered obsolete the horse cavalry, horse-drawn artillery, and the "straight-leg" foot-slogging infantry. Today, nearly all land mobility is accomplished on wheels or tracks. Except for some infantry and special forces, land warfare since WWII has been exclusively mechanized.

The tactics and strategies of mechanized warfare were devised over sixty years ago by the Germans—who developed the "air-land battle"—and then by the British Commonwealth, Soviet, and American armed forces that refined and perfected them. Land battles today are fundamentally similar to their historical predecessors. It's just that engagement ranges are farther, intelligence and air support are better, armor is thicker, and high-tech electronics add a greater degree of precision to many of the military tasks.

RIGHT: The German Army pioneered the concept of modern warfare as we know and practice it today–a concept based more on a force's ability to move quickly in a coordinated way. These troops ride a Zundapp motorcycle and sidecar near Smolensk, deep in Russia, in July 1941.

The vehicles pictured in this book are representative of combat, combat support, and combat service support vehicle systems. Some are in front-line military service, while others are in private and public collections.

These private collections are quite remarkable. In the past, only a few select museums bothered to preserve military equipment, and even fewer collected bulky and heavy items like tanks or trucks. Happily, that has changed. Additionally, the formal collections of armor and wheeled military vehicles have now been joined by thousands of private collectors all over Europe, North America, Australia, and New Zealand, where individuals acquire and restore scout cars, lorries, jeeps, and even armored cars and tanks.

One other thing: if American models seem to predominate here, it is because of a prolific arms industry during the past six decades. The American Sherman tank, the Studebaker truck, the Jeep, and many other military vehicles became standard equipment for Great Britain as well as the United States, and were used extensively by all the Allied armies, including the Soviets, during and after World War II.

WL-376784

FOOT INFANTRY AND HORSE-DRAWN ARTILLERY DOMINATED LAND WARFARE FOR HUNDREDS OF YEARS, UNTIL THE TIME OF THE FIRST WORLD WAR. DURING THAT TIME, THE STYLE OF BATTLE REMAINED THE SAME. HUGE NUMBERS OF SOLDIERS MANEUVERED AGAINST EACH OTHER, THEN CLOSED TO ABOUT 100 YARDS (91.4M) AND EXCHANGED VOLLEYS OF FIRE. THIS MUSKET FIRE WAS INACCURATE AND OFTEN INEFFECTIVE BEYOND 50 YARDS (45.7M). COMBAT WAS A PRIMITIVE BUSINESS, GENERALLY LASTING A FEW MINUTES OR A FEW HOURS, AND CONCLUDING WITH EITHER A ROUT OR HAND-TO-HAND BAYONET FIGHTING.

WITH THE ADVENT OF REPEATING RIFLES–DEVELOPED AND INTRODUCED IN THE LATTER PART OF THE NINETEENTH CENTURY–LAND WARFARE CHANGED. RIFLES BECAME ACCURATE AND DEADLY TO RANGES OF 500 YARDS (57.2M) AND MORE. A TRAINED RIFLEMAN COULD FIRE TWENTY OR MORE AIMED ROUNDS EVERY MINUTE. A WELL-TRAINED AND DUG-IN RIFLE PLATOON WITH FORTY-FOUR SOLDIERS COULD DOMINATE A SECTION OF TERRAIN WITH A HUGE VOLUME OF ACCURATE FIRE. AFTER THE INTRODUCTION OF SUCH RIFLES AND TACTICS APPROPRIATE TO THEIR USE, IT WAS, EFFECTIVELY, SUICIDE TO ASSAULT A POSITION HELD BY SUCH RIFLEMEN.

ANOTHER DEVELOPMENT THAT CHANGED THE NATURE OF LAND WARFARE CAME ALONG ABOUT THE SAME TIME: IMPROVED COMMUNICATIONS. PRIOR TO THE INTRODUCTION OF THE TELEGRAPH AND THEN THE TELEPHONE, ARTILLERY FIRE BEYOND LINE OF SIGHT WAS NOTORIOUSLY INACCU-

LEFT: The learning curve was steep for those early tankers and tank designers, with frequent breakdowns and disasters. But the effect of the basic concept on land warfare was immediate and profound.

RATE. THAT, TOO, CHANGED AROUND THE TIME OF WORLD WAR I.

THE RESULT WAS A KIND OF WARFARE THAT IS ALMOST UNIMAGINABLE, EVEN TODAY. WITH GOOD FIELD TELEPHONE OR TELEGRAPH COMMUNICATIONS BETWEEN A "FORWARD OBSERVER" AND AN ARTILLERY BATTERY FAR BEHIND THE LINES, VERY TIMELY AND ACCURATE FIRE COULD BE PLACED ON TARGETS. THIS MADE THE SOLDIER'S POSITION FAR MORE PRECARIOUS THAN IN PREVIOUS WARS. HUNDREDS OF THOUSANDS OF SOLDIERS DIED DURING THAT WAR IN INDIVIDUAL BATTLES–IN JUST A FEW DAYS–AND ACHIEVED NOTHING. THE WAR DETERIORATED TO A STALEMATE, WITH BOTH SIDES DUG IN AND IMMOBILE, RAPIDLY BEING BLED DRY.

THE TANK WAS DEVELOPED TO BREAK THIS STALEMATE, AND IT SUCCEEDED. THE FIRST TANKS WERE BRITISH, AND THEY WERE HELLISH MACHINES TO CREW. INSIDE IT WAS SO HOT THAT DRIVERS AND CREWMEN OFTEN FAINTED, SO NOISY THAT VOICE COMMUNICATION WAS IMPOSSIBLE. THEY WERE SLOW AND EXTREMELY UNRELIABLE, AND PROVIDED VERY LIMITED PROTECTION FROM EVEN SMALL-ARMS FIRE. THEIR MISSION WAS TO CROSS THE DEADLY NO-MAN'S-LAND AND ATTACK GERMAN INFANTRY ON THEIR OWN GROUND, GENERALLY IN SUPPORT OF INFANTRY ATTACKS. LATER IN THE WAR, ALL KINDS OF DESIGNS WERE TRIED; SOME WERE SUCCESSFUL, BUT MOST WERE NOT.

STILL, THE POWER OF THE ARMORED TANK WAS BEING REALIZED. WHEN USED INTELLIGENTLY, IN CONJUNCTION WITH ONE ANOTHER, TANKS WORKED MIRACLES. TANKS PUSHED THE BATTLE ONWARD, AND WARFARE WOULD NEVER RETURN TO THE MASSIVE, BLOODY STALEMATES OF THE TRENCH.

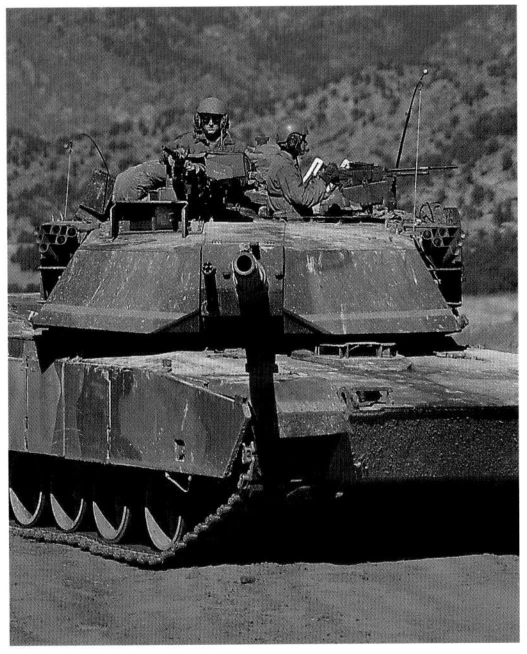

LEFT: The details of today's tanks are far more complex and costly, but the fundamental ideas are the same–mobile, protected firepower.

CHAPTER ONE

TANK BASICS

There are three fundamental characteristics to evaluate for every tank: firepower, mobility, and protection. All armored fighting vehicles feature varying combinations of these elements. Heavy tanks are designed to slug it out with equivalent enemy vehicles, while hit-and-run recon vehicles may have light armor protection but high mobility that enables them to dash for the exits if they bump up against an enemy tank.

FIREPOWER

Firepower is the product of a tank's two gun types: 1) machine-gun fire for use against infantry, light-skinned vehicles, and aircraft, and 2) heavier cannon fire for use against other tanks, bunkers, pillboxes, and fortifications.

In the early years, the machine gun was the only weapon on some tanks. The British Whippet medium tank had only four .303cal Hotchkiss machine guns. Other World War I models used large caliber weapons as well. The British Mark IV (Male) had two 57mm "6-pounder" (2.7kg) cannons, named for the weight of the projectiles they fired.

RIGHT: Heavy metal magic—the massive M60 main battle tank. BELOW: On the way! An M1A2 Abrams cuts loose with its marvelous 120mm smoothbore cannon.

Today, a tank's main guns are typically 120mm weapons so accurate that they are expected to hit a target over a mile (up to 2km) away on the first shot. They fire projectiles that fly across the battlefield faster than a mile (1.6km) per second and are capable of penetrating steel armor more than a foot (30.4cm) thick. Even lightly armored military vehicles today often have very high levels of firepower and mobility. This is the case with the light recon vehicles shown in this book mounting TOW missiles.

MOBILITY

Mobility is a tank's ability to move across terrain. The earliest tanks had a top speed of 3 mph (4.8kph)–walking speed. Of course, there is more to mobility than speed. A tank cannot be limited simply to where the road is. Tanks must travel soft ground, cross wide ditches and trenches, go over logs and other obstacles, and negotiate steep hillsides and grades. Even in the first years of tank warfare, tanks like the English Mk 1 Tank, Female, could cross 8-foot (2.4m) trenches and scale 4-foot (1.2m) parapets intended to impede them. Today, tanks cross ditches more than 10 feet (3m) wide, will reach speeds of 50 mph (80.4kph), and can climb and descend steep, slimy grades.

Mobility includes a concept tankers call "agility." It is amazing to see a massive vehicle roaring across open ground at high speed, then turning quickly to dash up a hill or down a narrow ravine. Modern tanks are more than fast; they accelerate and brake quickly, turn on a dime, and go just about anywhere.

In fact, most modern tanks can even go underwater. The Russians traditionally have placed great emphasis on the capability of their tanks to cross rivers unaided, by fording. The T-72 and many other main battle tanks (MBTs) can cross rivers up to 18 feet (5.4m) deep! That takes a little preparation–the onboard snorkel needs to be installed–but it is a common task for such tankers. The ability to ford a river is part of a tank's mobility and agility that can be as important as its firepower.

Moving a heavily armored vehicle takes lots of power, and finding suitable power plants and drivetrain components has always been a problem for tank designers. During WWII, tanks used dual engines, or a single engine assembled from several conventional engine blocks. Others used a massive air-cooled radial engine designed for an aircraft.

World War I tanks often used a V-12 (so called because of the twin banks of 6 cylinders in a "V" configuration) Liberty engine producing 338 horsepower (hp). By World War II, tank engine output was up to about

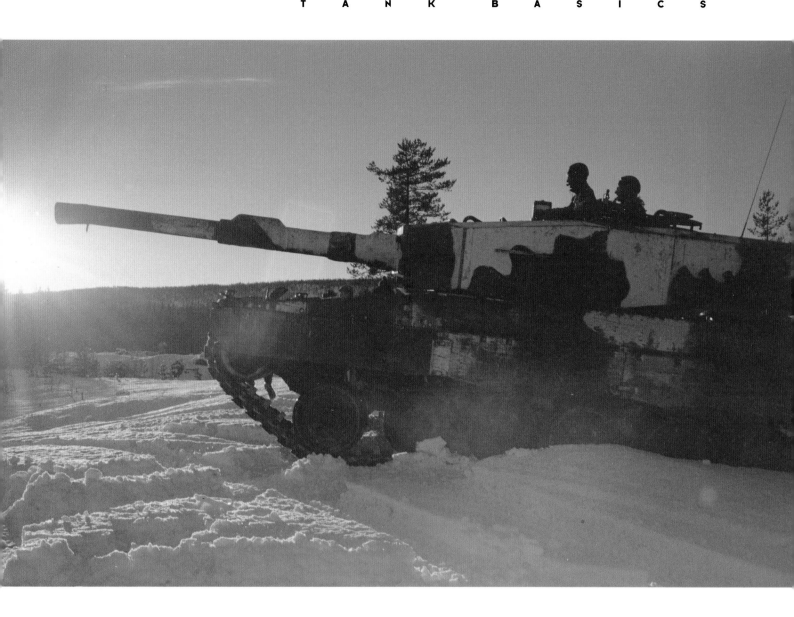

OPPOSITE: An Israeli tank commander and gunner scan for targets in the Golan Heights. Their superb Merkeva main battle tank is designed to provide extra protection for the crew and extra hazard for any enemy. **ABOVE:** Modern tank guns are extremely accurate to very long range—this crew can destroy almost any other tank with its first shot, anywhere within a mile (1.6km) or so. **RIGHT:** This power pack from a British Challenger MBT is typical of the most advanced contemporary tanks–tremendously powerful, reliable, and relatively fuel efficient.

500 hp for the U.S. Sherman and 700 hp for the German Tiger and Panther. The current M1 Abrams uses a 1500 hp gas turbine engine that moves the 70-ton (63.4t) vehicle along at speeds in excess of 45 mph (72.4kph).

PROTECTION

Protection is the tank's ability to keep its crew safe from hostile fire. This comes from 1) the thickness of the armor, 2) the tank's shape and design, and 3) the tank's evasive mobility.

Armor has evolved from simple ¼- and ½-inch (6 and 12mm) steel plate, designed to resist rifle fire, to today's exotic composite armor that may be up to 12 or more inches (30.4cm) in thickness. Modern armor can be made of depleted uranium—an extremely dense, tough material—as is the case with the M1 Abrams, or from "Chobham"-type composites as found on the British Challenger 2 and M1A2 Abrams. Although the exact nature of Chobham armor remains, after many years, a carefully guarded British secret, it is known that the material is a sandwich of materials, including metal and ceramic components, and is extremely resistant to anti-tank weapons.

The most common armor from World War II until the 1970s was made of cast- or rolled-steel alloys. While casting had a lot of advantages—variable thickness within a single component, and easily included complex curves—cast-steel armor wasn't as tough pound for pound as rolled-plate alloy. But it worked well enough for designers to incorporate castings for the crucial turret in the M60, the T-55, -62, and -72, as well as other common models.

The virtues of casting were apparent during World War II in the turret of the famous M4 Sherman. It had a single component with 4-inch (10.1cm) armor on the turret's forward surface, where most hits are likely to occur, and 2-inch (5cm) armor on the sides and rear. That saved weight, which was important considering protective armor accounted for half the weight of most tanks.

Protection against enemy fire is accomplished by more than just thick armor. In 1941 the Russians shocked the Germans with the introduction of the T-34 medium tank, a design that had superior firepower, mobility, and protection. The Germans panicked when they discovered that, when their tanks and anti-tank guns fired at the frontal armor of this new tank, almost everything bounced off. The T-34 was virtually invulnerable. Only the mobile 88mm dual-purpose gun, with its 21-pound (9.5kg) shells, was effective against it.

LEFT: This slender metal dart contains no explosives, but it can blast through the thickest armor. Commonly called a "sabot" round for the aluminum device surrounding it, this heavy projectile (made of depleted uranium) flies out of the muzzle of the gun at more than 5,000 feet (1,524m) per second. Its kinetic energy is all that is required to bore a hole through several feet of cast-steel armor. OPPOSITE: The M1 Abrams front surface armor is a composite of depleted uranium, ceramic, steel alloy, and other components. The exact nature of the material is a well-guarded secret. This armor proved to be highly effective at defeating everything the Iraqi Army fired at it, even at close range.

RIGHT: Here's what happens when an obsolete weapons technology meets something more advanced–100 tons (90.7t) of scrap metal. These 1960s-era Russian T-55s, and their demoralized Iraqi crews, were no match for more modern British and American main battle tanks. BELOW: Virtually all modern combat vehicles are the product of many years of development, highly technical machines that demand a very high level of training for the crew.

Russian technicians accomplished this virtual invulnerability by sloping the tank's armor at a carefully calculated angle that tended to deflect projectiles. This sloped armor improved protection without increasing weight. The principle was quickly adopted by most nations, although the style of design varied considerably.

The most modern of tanks today avoid the use of cast-steel armor–it is just too vulnerable to modern anti-tank weapons. During Operation Desert Storm, American tankers routinely destroyed Iraqi T-72s with high-velocity "sabot" rounds–nonexplosive, heavy steel darts that fly across the battlefield at about a mile (1.6km) per second. Sabot rounds have been known to cut right through the toughest, thickest cast armor, sometimes going right through the tank and coming out the other side. In fact, in one case, a sabot round went through a berm (a protective earth bank or mound) that was sheltering an Iraqi tank, then through the tank, and continued on through another berm on the far side of the vehicle.

The Iraqis got seven hits on M1 Abrams tanks in the same conflict, and none of those hits did any major damage. That's because the Abrams used a different kind of armor than the T-72: a variation on the Chobham principle of layered components plus steep angles on the armor faces, which effectively defeats most modern kinetic energy rounds.

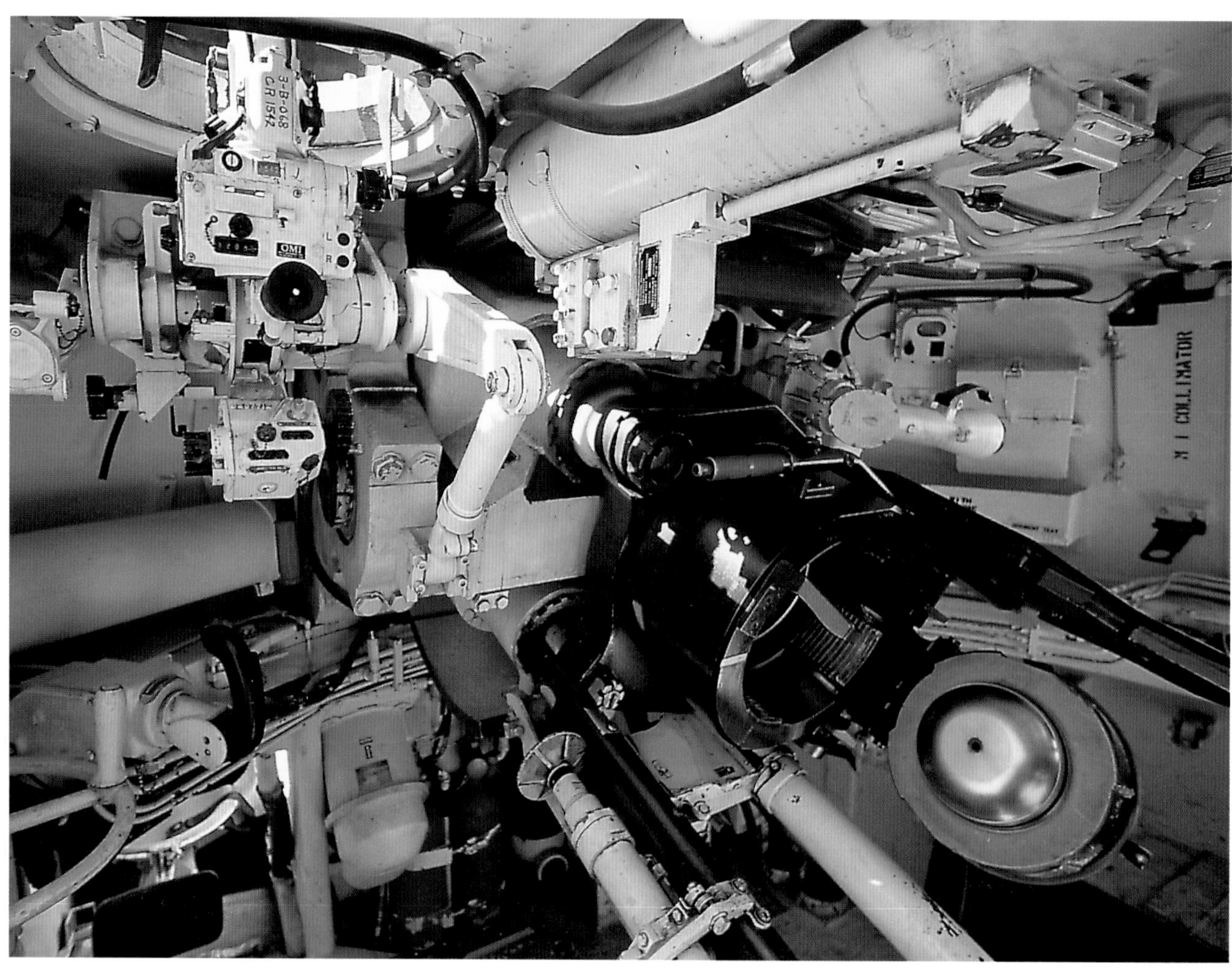

CHAPTER TWO

THE MATILDA

Today the Matilda looks like a somewhat small, vulnerable, under-gunned tank—smaller than an M2 Bradley and many other contemporary fighting vehicles. But back in her day, Matilda was quite a girl. In some important ways, this tough little tank helped win World War II.

The early battles of the European war were dominated by Germany, but that changed in 1940 after the legendary 7th Royal Tank Regiment waltzed into Libya with Matildas. The tank formally known as "The Infantry Tank, Mark II, Matilda II (A12)" saw her first action chasing the Axis across North Africa. She helped destroy the Italian Army that threatened Egypt and the Mediterranean.

Matildas and the 8th Army then helped hold the Afrika Korps at bay until bigger American M3 Lees and M4 Shermans arrived. Matilda's career as a frontline MBT was brief, but that doesn't mean it wasn't exciting. Her last major gunfight with massed enemy armor was in July 1942 at the Battle of Alamein. After that, the German Panzer PzKpfw IVs—with their bigger guns, high-explosive shells (which the Matilda lacked), and better armor and mobility—outclassed the Matilda, and she was withdrawn from her role as an MBT.

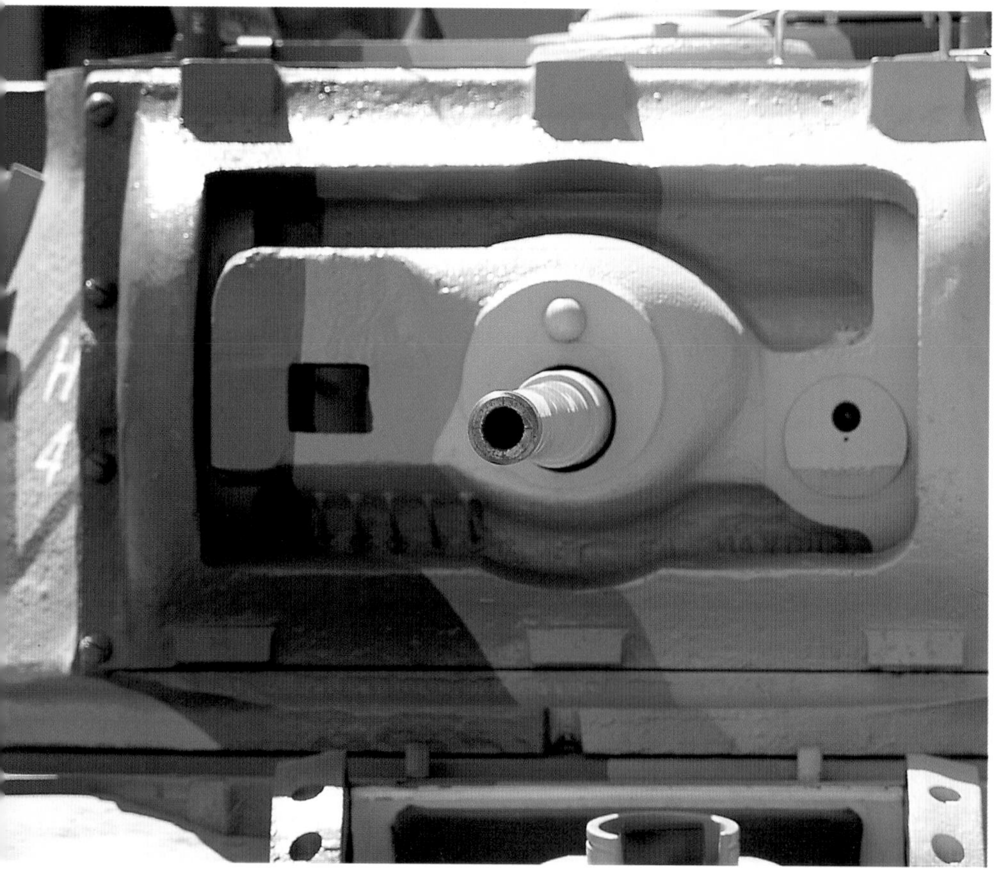

The Matilda was born in 1938 as an infantry-support tank. In those days, most armies fielded a tank designed as a kind of mobile pillbox to move along with the troops, guarding them from enemy armor. Her top speed didn't need to be very fast, and it wasn't: 15mph (24.1kph) was

as fast as she could move, and that was going downhill on a freshly paved road. Maximum speed was closer to 8 mph (12.8kph) when traveling cross-country.

But Matilda was a tough customer. Her hide was impervious to anything the Italians had to offer, and everything the PzKpfw IIIs fired as well. The track plates on each side of the hull are huge, massive plates of 1-inch (2.5cm) -thick armor. The turret and hull front surfaces are similarly massive, up to 3 inches (7.6cm) on the gun mantlet, and well armored all over. All that armor made for a

OPPOSITE: Detail, Matilda gun and mantlet. ABOVE: It looks small and insignificant today, but half a century ago the British Matilda heavy tank, with its 37mm cannon, held the Nazi horde at bay in many battles across France and North Africa.

LEFT: Even the Afrika Korps admired the Matilda, and they sometimes repaired damaged ones for their own use. Matilda's armor was impervious to anything the Germans could throw at it–until the Panzer IV came along.

heavy tank during the early days of World War II. When many tanks weighed 20 tons (18.1t), Matilda weighed 30 tons (27.2t).

The only practical way to propel the tank back in 1938 was to install a pair of engines. The first Mark I and II Matildas used a pair of AEC 6-cylinder diesels, originally designed for use in buses. Together, these two engines provided 174 hp and were very difficult to service and maintain. Later, Mark III Matildas used twin Leyland diesel engines producing 190 hp.

The Matilda's main gun, and its limiting factor after 1942, is a 40mm weapon called a "2-pounder" (908g). This weapon was a state-of-the-art cannon when it was designed in 1937, at the time one of the best anti-armor guns in any army. This weapon fired two standard projectiles, both useful only against armor: a solid armor-piercing (AP) round, and a similar armor-piercing-capped (APC) version. The AP projectile zipped down-range at 2,800 feet per second (fps) (853.4 meters per second) out of the muzzle and would penetrate 2¼ inches (5.7cm) of homogenous armor steel at 30 degrees. The APC's initial velocity was 2,600 fps (792.4 mps) and would penetrate 2⅓ inches (5.9mm). Those are impressive figures for the late 1930s–impressive enough that the gun was installed in two other new British tanks of that era, the Valentine and the Crusader.

OPERATION BATTLEAXE: JUNE 15, 1941

The Battle Diary of the German 8th Machine-gun Battalion describes how eight Matildas and infantry came in to attack them:

Once again our 37mm Pak is powerless. Its shells just bounce off the tank's thick armor; only a lucky shot in its tracks or turret bearings has any effect. So they rumble on to within 100 yards [91.4m] of our position, halt and then knock out our Paks one by one. We watch bitterly as one gun after another stops firing. Even individual acts of gallantry cannot help in this situation. Gunner Blank of 7 Co. is still firing on a Matilda at five yards [4.5m] range: no good. The steel colossus rolls on over him and his gun. His comrades bring the brave young lad back to us, our surgeon has to amputate both legs on the battlefield because they are just pulp. Later he died of his injuries.

GEORGE BRADFORD ON THE MATILDA

GEORGE R. BRADFORD is the editor of *AFV News*, a military vehicle enthusiast's magazine published in Canada. Here's what he has to say about Matilda.

Nearly three thousand infantry tanks—Mk II Matildas—of all types participated in World War II, from North Africa to the Pacific, and through Lend-Lease, with Russian forces. However, their tour of duty in the Western Desert battles would have to be deemed their glory days. Earlier, a few Matilda IIs had reached France in 1940, and made themselves known. As the war came to an end, Matildas were still in use by the Australians on Borneo.

Initially, its 3-inch (7.6mm) frontal armor stymied almost all enemy anti-tank guns. Only the German FlaK 36 with its 88mm gun had success against them.

The Matilda II was designed to support infantry advances, and as such had a top speed of 15 mph (24.1kph), which was often not fast enough to counter enemy armor moves in the desert. However, they could withstand all the incoming fire the enemy could muster—and at the same time, their 2-pounder (908g) AP gun could penetrate most early-war enemy armor. This gun, however, would soon become hopelessly outranged by improved German tank weapons.

The Matilda is basically a complex "cast metal" tank with no basic frame. Since mass-production welding techniques were imperfect at this time, the cast-steel sections were bolted together through tapped holes to produce an extremely rigid structure. These hull and turret castings required precision tooling, making mass production a labor-intensive and slow process. However, the end result was an almost impregnable support tank

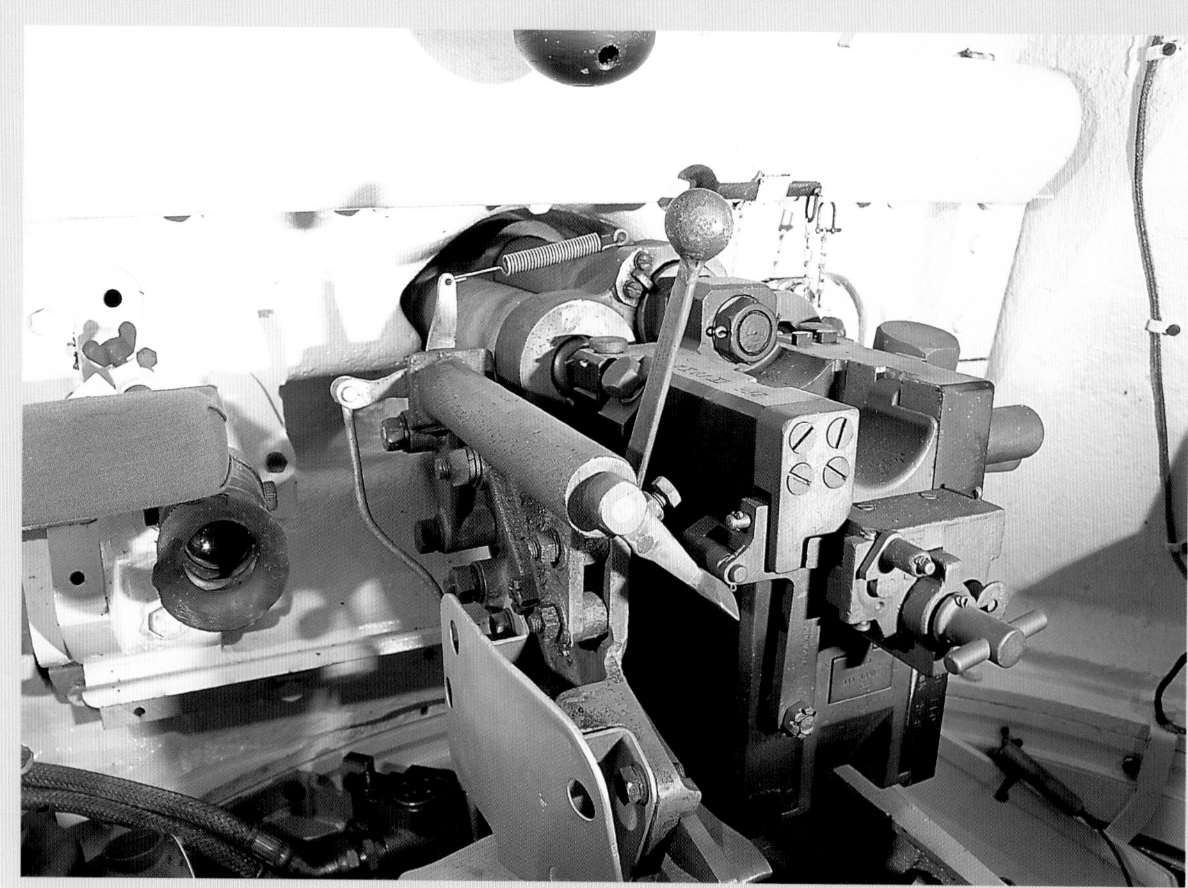

that effectively dominated the battlefield during the early British victories against the Italians in Libya.

The driver sits forward, and the other three crew members are suspended in the turret turntable, which runs on rollers over the floor of the fighting compartment. The commander sits to the rear left of his gunner and in the early models had a 12-inch (30.4cm) -high cupola with viewing slits. This high commander's cupola was gradually replaced by a much lower version with no viewing slits.

One of the main failings of the Matilda II was its main gun, which could fire only AP rounds, and thus was unable to support its infantry with high-explosive (HE) fire against soft targets like machine-gun positions, or effectively neutralize anti-tank positions for its own protection. Its comparatively slow speed also relegated it to cautious advances, since it could be easily outflanked by the faster German medium tanks on open terrain.

In action, a Matilda tank company was attached to an infantry brigade for a particular mission. They would precede the infantry in the assault stage with close support from Bren Carriers (light armored vehicles) of that unit, followed by the infantry on foot.

There were few mechanical weaknesses in the Matildas, short of the steering clutches failing, but their power turrets could be jammed by shell splinters or hits on the turret ring area. Naturally, thrown or damaged tracks could easily immobilize these heavy tanks, and many were captured and put into German service in North Africa.

By the time of the final Alamein offensives in late 1942, the Matilda had been relegated to the lowly chore of mine clearing, as the Matilda Scorpion was fitted with the rotary flail device.

OPPOSITE: Breech for Matilda's 37mm cannon.
ABOVE: The Matilda's 37mm muzzle. The marks are used by the crew during bore-sighting procedures, aligning the center of the tube with the gun's sights.

C H A P T E R   T H R E E

THE M3 AND M5 STUART

The Stuart tank, with its diminutive 37mm gun, is a good example of what a tank was supposed to be back in the late 1930s. At that time, a 37mm gun and 1-inch (2.5cm) armor were considered adequate for combat. And they were, too, for a few years. Early in the war, a 37mm gun was strong enough to puncture German Panzer IIIs and light armor in Europe, many Italian tanks and vehicles in North Africa, and all Japanese armor in the Pacific.

By 1943 and the advent of the Panzer IV, the Stuart no longer had any business going head to head with German MBTs. It soldiered on, though, in North Africa and across Europe, serving as a scout vehicle or manning roadblocks and checkpoints. If enemy trucks or infantry showed up, the Stuart could beat them up with its cannon and machine guns. If a Panzer IV or Tiger came around the corner, the Stuart could use its superior mobility to scoot quickly to safety. But a German 88mm high-velocity antitank projectile would slice right through a Stuart from front to back without slowing down.

Out in the Pacific, though, the Stuart light tank remained a valuable weapon. Not only did it fit neatly in landing-ship tanks (LSTs) for delivery to enemy beaches–at places like Guadalcanal, Peleliu, Iwo Jima, and Okinawa–but the Stuart's machine guns and flamethrowers were just what the general ordered for supporting the marines and army infantry fighting hordes of Japanese in the jungle. While Japanese tanks knocked out some Stuarts, artillery and satchel charges were a more common problem.

Despite some limitations and handicaps, the Stuart was a durable, successful combat vehicle for both the U.S. and British forces, and served right through to the end of the war. The Brits liked it so much that it was nicknamed the "Honey" by the Desert Rats in appreciation for its many excellent qualities, and they howled in protest when ordered to turn them in for newer tanks.

DESCRIPTION

The Stuart is officially a light tank, designed for a cavalry role. Though its firepower and protection are both limited, its mobility is excellent.

Fully tricked out with ammunition, full tanks, and a well-fed crew, the Stuart weighs only 16½ tons (15t), less than the gun on some more modern tanks. That lightness comes from a combination of the vehicle's compact size and the extensive use of lightweight components, including armor. Most of the vehicle is assembled from sheet steel and riveted or

LEFT: Detail of the Stuart's .30cal bow machine gun. This weapon was not very effective–the gunner's visibility and field of fire are both quite limited. OPPOSITE: The little Stuart was a fast, light, agile tank that was outclassed by German tanks early in the war. But it soldiered on, across Africa and Europe, scouting and providing support for the infantry, as one is doing here in France late in the war.

welded, with a casting for part of the hull. Cast armor became standard later in the war, but the little Stuart made do with the cut-and-paste technology of an earlier age.

The armor on the early Stuarts is amazingly thin: about 1 inch (2.5cm) on the upper hull glacis plate, angled at 48 degrees, 17⅓ inches (44 cm) on the lower cast portion of the hull, and ⅓ to 1 inch (76mm–2.5cm) on the rest of the hull. The turret's gun shield is 2 inches (5cm) thick, the front surface is 1½ inches (3.8cm) thick, and the sides are a little more than an inch thick (2.5cm). By contrast, modern tanks offer around 1 foot (30.4cm) or more of armor on the glacis plate, and angle it at 60 degrees or more—doubling its protection value.

WEAPONRY

A 37mm M6 gun in an M23 mount provides the primary armament for the Stuart, with a hydraulic motor supplying powered traverse and a manual backup. With the power traverse energized, the gunner can rotate the

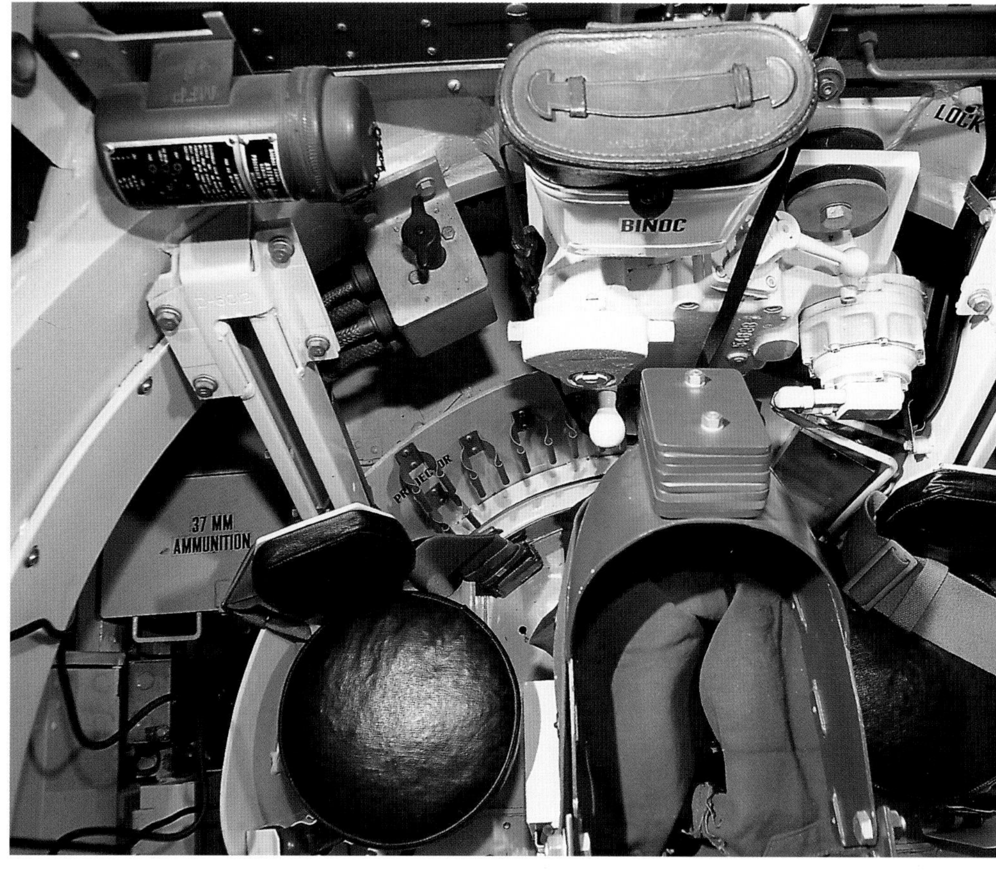

OPPOSITE: It looks factory-fresh, but this is actually a privately owned and perfectly restored fifty-year-old M5. The weapons won't fire, but everything else is in new condition. RIGHT: Looking down into the turret of the Stuart. That's the commander's seat on the left; the gun breech is in the lower center of the photograph.

turret a full 360 degrees in fifteen seconds. The tube can elevate to +20 degrees and depress to -10. A good crew can pop off thirty rounds per minute, but at that rate they would go through all their ammunition in about four minutes. One hundred twenty-three rounds of 37mm ammo were stowed in the M5 version. Racks throughout the tank held 420 rounds for the M1928A1 Thompson machine guns and 6,250 rounds for the M1919A5 co-axial machine gun in the turret, the M1919A4 on the turret roof, and the 1919A4 bow gun. For those really tough encounters with the enemy, there were twelve hand grenades to toss out of the turret hatch in the event that swarming infantry attempted to board.

The gunner got his overview of the battlefield through a small M4 periscope and a small M38 telescopic sight for aligning the co-axial, or "co-ax." He aimed the main gun with an M40 telescopic sight. No range finder was installed, so he had to make an educated guess at the range. The main gun had a primitive but useful early vertical axis stabilization system—similar to that of a home video camera—to keep the weapon aimed approximately on target while the tank rocked and rolled across the terrain. This stabilizer didn't lock the gun onto the target—that would come later—but it did a fairly effective job of keeping it pointed in the right direction, regardless of the motion of the tank as it waddled over the ground. The control for the stabilization system was on the left turret wall, above the controls for the gun. A control grip on the left of the gunner's position allowed him to traverse the gun under power. Two red buttons on the grip permitted him to fire the main gun and the co-ax machine gun without having to look away from the M4 sight.

Visibility for the gunner and crew is very limited. The driver and the assistant driver/bow machine gunner are allowed only a peephole slot and an M6 periscope to see where they are going. The commander can stick his head out of the hatch, open one of the pistol ports, or use his M6 periscope. He also has two vision blocks (thick glass viewing devices that provided some measure of protection against small-arms fire and artillery fragments), called Protectoscopes by the manufacturer. Little wonder that the crews fought with the hatches open as much as possible.

Rounds for the little gun are about the size of a twelve-ounce (340g) Coke bottle, and would be about as effective against a modern tank. Four kinds of projectiles were in common use: M51 APC, M74 AP, M63 HE, and M2 Canister. The AP rounds naturally have the highest velocity (2,900 fps [883.9mps] for the M51) and carry the farthest (12,850 yards [11, 750m]). Although the round will

fly about 7 miles (11.2km) down-range, it is only effective against armor at ranges inside a mile (1.6km). It can penetrate a little more than 2 inches (5cm) of steel at 500 yards (457.2m), and only about 1½ inches (3.8cm) at 2,000 yards (1828.8m). The canister round is a kind of shot-gun shell on steroids, designed for use against people. It contained 122 steel pellets, each about ¼ inch (6mm) in diameter and lethal only inside 200 yards (182.8m).

POWER TRAIN

The M5 Stuart has two Cadillac engines for propulsion. (The M3 version used an air-cooled radial.) The M5's power train has proved to be strong, simple, and dependable. These engines, both big 8-cylinder Series 42 power plants, use 80-octane gasoline and generate up to 296 hp, depending on the version in use.

That is a pretty good power-to-weight ratio. The M5 will zoom along at 36 mph (57.9kph) on a level road, climb a 60 percent grade, and cross a ditch more than 5 feet (1.5m) wide. It can climb an 18-inch (45.7cm) wall and ford a creek 3 feet (91.4cm) deep. Filled up, with 89 gallons (336.8L) of gas aboard, the Stuart has a range of about 100 miles (160.9km). That's only a little over 1 mile per gallon (mpg) (1.6km per 3.7L), yet still pretty good fuel economy for a tank.

OPPOSITE: **A Stuart pauses during war games about 1941 to salute the passing commander. There were high hopes for the little tank at the time, but its thin armor and small gun were quickly made obsolete by German Panzers.**

One pleasing factor for the M5 Stuart driver is the hydramatic transmission, a 2-speed unit that greatly eases the workload on the guy up front. It is a big improvement on the M3's 5-speed synchromesh tranny. Until quite recently, managing the gears on nearly all tanks—while simultaneously wrestling with the steering laterals—required strength, endurance, and coordination. The Stuart driver, however, gets a little bonus from the vehicle's designer; maybe that's why they called it Honey.

Each M5 Stuart came equipped with an M238 flag set for signaling, a spotlight, a siren, and at least one radio set—SCR 508, 528, or 538. Command tanks had a SCR 506 in the left sponson as well. Command tanks were also issued a flare set (M17 and M18, three each) and a ground signal projector.

COMBAT HISTORY

The Stuart didn't get to be nearly as famous as its bigger brother, the M4 Sherman medium tank, but it played a significant role in preparing American forces for armored combat in World War II. It was the first American-designed-and-built tank to fire shots in combat.

ANOTHER MK IV BITES THE DUST

The following anecdote was provided courtesy of Aaron Elson, author of *Tanks for the Memories*, an oral history of the U.S. Army 712th Tank Battalion. Its source is a note on the back of an ancient After Action Review (AAR), a report written immediately following combat. The author of the note is Sgt. Max Lutcavish, a tank commander from D Company, 712th Tank Battalion, describing a rare and lucky victory of a Stuart over a Mk V Panzer. While in a light tank platoon's lead vehicle, moving up a road northeast from Alencon, France, the following action took place on August 12, 1944:

Upon rounding a curve, we suddenly came upon an enemy truck loaded with Germans. Before my gunner, Cpl. O'Farrell, could fire, the truck stopped and backed around the curve. We pursued it and directed fire with the 37mm and co-axial guns at a group of dismounted Germans by their truck. About that time I heard a terrific explosion. I looked to the rear and the tank directly behind me was in flames. I caught a glimpse of a whirl of dust caused by a muzzle blast to my right. Immediately I spotted the position under an apple tree at about 125 yards (114.3m) away.

I didn't know for sure what it was or whether it could be knocked out with my 37mm. But I knew I had to do something quick because it was already traversing its gun onto me. There was no cover or no way to go back because of the burning tank behind me. Again I heard an explosion and felt my tank lunge forward. A bazooka had hit me in the rear and set the rear end of the tank on fire. What a position for a churchgoing man to be in!

There was nothing else to do but to dish it out, so I directed fire on the gun position that looked like that of a tank. That gunner of mine was plenty fast. In less time than it takes to tell he threw eight well-placed rounds of AP into that position and had it on fire. Now we could definitely tell it was a tank, a huge one with a gun that made our 37 look like a pea-shooter.

While we were wiping the cold sweat from our brow, another enemy tank crossed the road about 400 yards (365.7m) ahead of us. We swung the turret in that direction hoping that we could chalk up another one, but the tank disappeared in the brush before the gunner could fire on it. By this time my tank was burning badly so I ordered the crew to abandon it—disregarding the numbers system, and we made our way back to the rest of the Platoon, toot-sweet, on foot.

M2A4 Stuarts were the very best and most modern tanks available to the U.S. Army in the late 1930s and early 1940s. They were used extensively for training and for large-scale war games. The Armored Force war games were conducted, circa 1941, in Louisiana, Tennessee, the Carolinas, and the Mojave Desert. Some Stuarts were delivered to Britain that year and were used for training there, too. They allowed armor unit commanders and crewmen to learn their trade, and they learned it well.

World War II came to Britain in September 1939, more than two years before Pearl Harbor. During those two long years, England and the Commonwealth nations battled Nazi Germany and Fascist Italy pretty much alone. In July 1941, the first shipment of American M3s arrived in North Africa to replace British combat losses. This first batch of Stuarts went to the 8th King's Royal Irish Hussars, followed by shipments to the 3rd and 5th Royal Tank Regiments of the 4th Armoured Tank Brigade.

The Brits had misgivings initially about the layout of the Stuart's fighting compartment and its weapons, but were soon enthusiastic converts. The U.S. tanks went into battle on November 18, 1941, as part of Operation Crusader. The Stuarts proved to be fast and reliable in the harsh desert, even if they were undergunned.

Stuarts went off to Burma with the Brits, too, in 1942, with a contingent from the 7th Armoured Brigade–Desert Rats about to be converted to Jungle Rats. The M3s also fought well in the jungle, and with little Japanese armor to worry about, the Stuarts performed extremely well against enemy infantry.

Americans first used the Stuart in combat in December 1942, against the Japanese on Luzon, in the Philippines, by the U.S. Army's 192nd

OPPOSITE: Stuarts in Italy, part of a Free French unit. They will run and hide if a Mk V or VI Panzer appears, but otherwise they can provide excellent support for infantry crawling up these muddy hills.

and 194th Tank Battalions, both National Guard units. Inexperienced, badly equipped, and poorly trained, the tankers fought a valiant rear-guard defense against the Japanese as U.S. forces retreated to Bataan for a final stand. All the tanks, as well as the tankers, were lost to the Japanese, but some lessons had been learned about how tanks could be used in close combat, about coordination with infantry, and about operating in the jungle.

While the Japanese were busy mopping up the survivors on Baatan and trying to figure out how to use the Stuarts for their own army, other Stuarts were going ashore on the far side of the globe, in North Africa at Casablanca and Oran, battling Vichy French tanks. American tank forces were finally fighting the Axis during Operation Torch. The M3s did well against the old French armor that their crews encountered in the campaign's first phase.

They didn't do as well against the Panzerkampfwagen (PzKpfw) IIIs and IVs encountered by 1st Battalion, 1st Armored Regiment, in the Chouigui Pass. There, on November 26, 1942, the unit encountered Germans from the 190th Panzer Battalion. In the ensuing fight, six Stuarts were destroyed. In return, six PzKpfw IVs and one PzKpfw I were knocked out, but only because the Panzers exposed themselves to rear shots and took multiple hits through their thin engine doors.

This combat proved that the Stuarts were outclassed by enemy medium tanks; from then on, the Stuart's role was generally restricted to fast, light reconnaissance–a job it did quite well in Europe for the duration of the war.

Stuarts played a more active role in the Pacific. There, enemy forces never fielded medium tanks. Soldiers and Marines seldom had any tanks to worry about at all. M3A1, M3A4, and Stuarts went ashore on Guadalcanal in 1942, supporting infantry, and performed very well. They hopped from island to island westward across the Pacific–New Georgia, Bougainville, Tarawa, Iwo Jima, Okinawa, and all the other exotic, legendary locales of the Pacific War.

Amazingly, the ancient little Stuart, in M3 and M5 versions, is still listed in service with many nations, including Chile, Mexico, Haiti, Guatemala, and Paraguay.

SPECIFICATIONS	M5A1 Stuart Light Tank
Crew	4
Weight	33,100 lbs (15t)
Length with gun forward	14 ft 6⅘ in (4.4m)
Turret height	8 ft 6 in (2.5m)
Width	7 ft 4 3/10 in (2.2m)
Ground clearance	16.5 in (41.9cm)
Ground pressure	12.2 lbs (5.5kg)
Propulsion	Twin Series 42 Cadillac water-cooled gasoline engine, 16 cylinders combined, displacing 692 cubic inches; 220 hp total at 3400 rpm
Transmission	Hydramatic; four forward, one reverse gear
Maximum governed speed	36 mph (57.9kph)
Range	100 miles (160.9km) on paved road
Obstacle crossing	Vertical: 18 in (45.7cm) Trench: 5.3 ft (1.6m)
Main armament	37mm Gun M6 in Mount M23
Co-axial weapon	.30cal M1919A5
Loader's weapon	.30cal M1919A4
Commander's weapon	.30cal M1919A4

CHAPTER FOUR

DIE PANZER

Military technology and history enthusiasts still have mixed feelings about Germany's systems and soldiers in World War II. The German army was undoubtedly the best organized, equipped, trained, and disciplined force of its time. It had some of the very best weapons, tactics, and leaders. The tragedy of this army–and its largely honorable soldiers–was that it was used for evil purposes. Even so, the German army of that war set the standard and designed the pattern for today's American army. Germany's WWII tanks continue to inspire today's tank designers. Thus the Panzers, despite their tragic origins, as both tank designs and combat organizations are tremendously important to understanding land combat today.

ABOVE: Panzer Mk IIs were adequate during the opening battles of World War II but were quickly outclassed and blown away by British Matildas, American Stuarts, and most other tanks on the battlefield. OPPOSITE: A Mk III is unloaded somewhere in North Africa, ready to change the rules of the game.

PANZER III

In 1933 Germany began rebuilding its military capability, based on the lessons learned in World War I, and on the visionary writing of an English soldier, Liddell Hart, who wrote extensively after the war about the future use of armor in warfare. The new, self-sufficient German army was designed as a highly mobile integration of tanks, troops, ground attack aviation, and artillery. The Panzers were the foundation of what the U.S. Army today calls a "combined arms team."

Early models of the breed, called the Panzerkampfwagen (PzKpfw) I and II, were developed in the mid-1930s. These light tanks were intended more for training than combat. The armament on the PzKpfw I was no more than twin machine guns. The PzKpfw II mounted 20mm and 7.62mm machine guns. Both were lightweight interim designs with interim objectives. The real tanks were, at that time, still on the drawing boards and on the test tracks. Even so, the PzKpfw II got a workout in Poland and France.

The PzKpfw III was the first combat-ready version of the series, an approximate equivalent to the British Matilda. It was issued to the tank battalions in 1939. The Mark III was an infantry support tank, designed to go up against other tanks. The first prototypes rolled out of the Daimler-Benz factory in 1936 and mounted a

37mm cannon. A bigger gun had been specified initially, but the smaller one was installed to conform to the caliber of Germany's other antitank guns. Like the Stuart, the PzKpfw III was eventually surpassed by bigger, better tanks by 1942, but would continue to serve till the end of the war.

The Mark III was a relatively small tank: 18 feet (5.4m) long, 9 feet (2.7m) wide, and only 7 feet (2.1m) high. That's extremely compact compared to its contemporaries, particularly the big M4 Sherman. Early versions of the Mark III weighed about 16 tons (14.5t), later ones up to 25 tons (22.6t).

The typical, midwar Mark III Ausf D (or D model) had a Maybach HL 108 TR V-12 gasoline engine generating 250 hp at 3000 rpm, more than sufficient muscle for a vehicle weighing 21 tons (19t). The result was a fast tank that could glide down the Autobahn at 25 mph (40.2kph) or across the pastoral French landscape

at about 11 mph (17.6kph). Cruising range on the Mark III D was 103 miles (165.7km). It could climb a 2-foot (61cm) obstacle, cross a trench about 7 feet (2.1m) wide, and go up a 30-degree slope. Those are pretty standard figures for most tanks of that day–and today, too.

One of the excellent features of the original Mark III Ausf A design was a large turret and turret ring, both intended to allow larger and better main guns in future models. Although the first Mark IIIs mounted a little 37mm cannon–and it was a good gun for targets of the era–the tank's gun grew, beginning with the Ausf E, into a 50mm cannon. Later versions, beginning with the Ausf M, got an even bigger 75mm gun, but the new gun suffered from a low-velocity design, as it was intended for close support rather than anti-armor targets.

The Ausf E was accepted for service just in time for the invasion of Poland in September 1939. Ninety-eight Mark IIIs participated in the operation. By the time the invasion of France and the low countries kicked off in May 1940, the *Wehrmacht* had 350 of all versions, primarily the Ausf E. That number had increased to fifteen hundred in 1941, and to forty-one hundred by the end of 1942.

Many of these were sent to North Africa and Rommel's legendary Afrika Korps. It was here that the PzKpfw III's deficiencies became apparent. Although the machine was fast and roomy, its firepower was inadequate for the challenges of desert warfare and the thick armor of British Matildas

LEFT: Up-gunned PzKpfw Mk IIIs ready for inspection, somewhere in Germany. **RIGHT:** Mk III Panzers halt along a railway during fighting in Greece. **BELOW:** Large numbers of Mk IIIs helped the Afrika Korps achieve a lasting reputation for combat effectiveness and efficiency–but against infantry, not other tanks.

and Valentines. The British 2-pounder (908g) gun could puncture the III's thin, 1⅕-inch (3cm) frontal armor, and the German tank couldn't return the favor until the 50mm cannons were issued. While these weapons were effective against the Matilda and Valentine, they were not at all effective against the Russian T-34's frontal and side armor, much to the dismay and panic of the German soldiers and commanders.

Despite its deficiencies, the Mark III was an adequate tank for its day, well designed to accommodate a long series of improvements. The combined weight of the bigger gun and heavier armor, however, ultimately made the vehicle too heavy for its power plant. Designers had originally left room in the turret for a bigger gun, but they hadn't anticipated a bigger engine. This proved to be the Mark III's major limitation.

Toward the end of the war, the Mark IIIs served in the second echelons and in support roles, relegated to combat in combination with light armor and infantry. Almost all Mark IIIs were destroyed in combat. The rare survivors went, almost without exception, to the scrap heap. If you want to see one, you may have to do some traveling. One restored and running Mark III is displayed at the British Tank Museum in Bovington, England, and a handful are in museums in Moscow, Russia, in Paris, France, and at the Patton Museum at Fort Knox, Kentucky.

ABOVE: An early PzKpfw IV, apparently in Poland during the September 1939 invasion. The short-barreled 75mm howitzer was quickly replaced with a higher-velocity model. **LEFT:** Driver's compartment, PzKpfw IV. **OPPOSITE:** Late-model PzKpfw Mk IVs with anti-bazooka plates. The Mk IV and its high-velocity 75mm gun was the mainstay of German forces till the end of World War II.

PANZER IV

A lot of tank designs emerged from World War II, including some remarkably durable ones. The Mark IV, for example, was in production for ten years, and in service–with one army or another–for more than thirty years.

German military doctrine called for armored battalions to have two types of tanks: most commonly, one that used a high-velocity gun for destroying armor (i.e., the Mark III in the early years); and, in addition, one that mounted a big gun, fired powerful HE rounds against bunkers and fortifications, and provided support for the assault. The Mark IV was designed for this role.

Early Mark IV Ausf Ds were about 19 feet (5.7m) long, 9½ feet (2.8m) wide, and 8½ feet (2.5m) high, and weighed about 22 tons (20t) combat loaded. They required a five-man crew, including a bow machine gunner/assistant driver. The heaviest armor (90mm) was on the front surfaces, but the front wasn't well sloped and could be penetrated by high-velocity rounds from even 40mm cannon, such as those found on the British Matilda. Mark IV armor melted like butter under the hot impact of 75mm or 85mm AP rounds from a Russian T-34, a major problem for German forces invading Russia.

A Maybach HL120 TRM V-12 gasoline engine provided 300 hp for the Mark IV D. It was coupled to the excellent "preselect" transmission used in many German WWII tanks. For its day the Mark IV was a fast tank–25 mph (40.2kph) on the road, about 13 mph (20.9kph) cross-country.

Several gun systems were installed on Mark IVs, but the D model used a 75mm KwK L/24 main gun. Eighty rounds for this cannon were stowed in the fighting compartment and in bins inside the hull. A co-axial MG 34 7.62mm machine gun was mounted to the right of the main gun, and twenty-eight hundred rounds for this weapon and the bow gun were also stowed in the hull. While the Mark

LEFT: Sometime before the D-Day invasion, a German tank crew rumbles down a quiet French street. **RIGHT:** An infantry patrol prowls past the corpse of a long-barreled PzKpfw Mk IV in the battered French town of Pontfaroy.

III's turret was traversed by hand, the IV used an electric power traverse.

One excellent feature of the whole long line of PzKpfw IV tanks was the tank commander's (TC) cupola. While many tanks of the era tried to give TCs good visibility under armor, the Mark IV was among the best, with good 360-degree observation from within a short cylinder at the turret rear. Another excellent feature was a pair of emergency escape hatches on the sides of the turret. These weakened the side armor yet more than compensated by allowing the commander, gunner, and loader to bail out much faster than the crews of most other tanks.

As with any long-lasting system, the Mark IV went through many upgrades, each normally resulting in a new model designation. The first major upgrade for the Mark IV was the D model. The D was used in the assaults on Poland and France at the outset of World War II, and then in Russia in 1941. The D's rather thin armor and 50mm gun were barely adequate to combat lighter enemy opposition, and clearly inadequate for combat with even the British Matilda and other potential opponents.

Then, with the coming of the E model, the Mark IV began to shine. Beginning in 1943 a new, long-barreled 75mm cannon (the KwK 40 L/48) was installed. This was one of the war's best tank guns. It was able to easily defeat most MBTs. It could even defeat the feared T-34/85 that had inspired such panic within the German Army two years earlier.

More than eight thousand PzKpfw IV tanks were built during the war. For a while, they helped Rommel drive the British in North Africa back into Egypt. Then Allied tankers and commanders learned how to deal with them by avoiding head-to-head engagements, by swarming individual enemy tanks, and by using their superior maneuverability to make shots from the flanks and rear, where their weapons were more effective. The Mark IVs were pushed back in turn, this time by a swarm of Shermans flying British colors.

The Mark IV fought well wherever it was sent: across Russia to the very gates of Moscow, and back again; across North Africa; into France; and then slowly back to Berlin, fighting a stubborn rear-guard battle all the way. The surviving tanks were durable enough to keep soldiering on long afterward, utilized by Syria against Israel in the 1967 war.

THE SOVIET T-34: THE PEOPLE'S TANK

The T-34 was probably the most prolific tank design in history, with many thousands built and some still in service half a century after its christening.

The T-34 was spectacularly successful during World War II—so much so that after the war the tank was sold in the tens of thousands to many emerging nations around the world, much to the dismay of the United States and NATO nations.

THE T-34 IN WORLD WAR II

When the Soviet T-34 arrived on the battlefield to confront German Panzers for the first time, in June 1941, the first reaction of the Nazis was surprise at the sight of this fast, low tank. That surprise was quickly followed by shock, then absolute panic, as the Germans discovered that nothing they had—except the excellent and legendary 88mm gun—could defeat the T-34's armor. AP rounds from the 50mm and 75mm guns on the early Panzer IIIs and IVs just bounced off and whizzed away. German commanders reported wholesale panic among the troops and Germany very seriously considered building exact copies as an emergency measure.

The Germans recovered their nerve, though, when inexperienced and incompetent Soviet commanders, using the T-34s piecemeal as infantry support, squandered the T-34's marvelous qualities. Learning how to deal with T-34s, the Germans defeated them by the hundreds by using the same basic techniques the Allies had used against the Mk IV, plus the murderous fire of the famous FlaK 88mm gun.

Yet new T-34s kept appearing on the battlefield, commanded by progressively better TCs, small unit leaders, and generals. The Soviets churned out T-34s by the thousands, from workshops and factories all over the vast nation, then threw them into battle. As the Soviets adjusted to the art of armored warfare, the T-34 began to dominate the eastern front, slowly pushing the vast German war

RIGHT: A German soldier rummages through the driver's compartment of an early T-34. OPPOSITE: Probably the best all-around tank of World War II, the Russian T-34 with its high-velocity 85mm gun combined firepower, mobility, and protection in one neat package. This one has been restored by Jacques Littlefield.

machine back toward Berlin, where it finally would be slain in May 1945. In the process, the T-34 became the first really modern tank, the model for just about everything since.

DESCRIPTION

Several features made the T-34 a war winner. There was an excellent 85mm gun installed on later models of the tank. The T-34 had a big, simple, powerful, reliable, oil-drinking V-12 diesel engine that developed 500 hp at 1800 rpm. It propelled the T-34 at good speed across snow, ice, mud, dust, and wide-open steppe. The feature that really got the Germans' attention, however, was the armor. It was thick—½ inch to 2⅓ inches (1.2 to 5.9cm)—and artfully sloped to deflect projectiles.

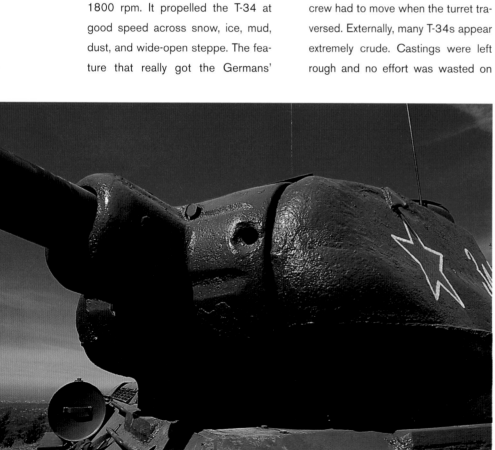

The T-34 is a fairly simple tank, and that is another of its virtues. It was designed to be built quickly and in vast numbers. From 1940 to 1945, forty thousand of them were manufactured. The turret of the T-34/85 was spacious, compared with its contemporaries, but it lacked a basket so the crew had to move when the turret traversed. Externally, many T-34s appear extremely crude. Castings were left rough and no effort was wasted on anything that wasn't important to the tank's ability to fight successfully.

RIGHT: An early T-34 after capture by the German Army in Russia, sometime in 1941. The turret was too small to accommodate the gun recoil mechanism, leaving it exposed and vulnerable. BELOW: The T-34's cast turret has marvelously shaped armor. This beautifully restored example is from Jacques Littlefield's collection.

While the American M4 Sherman loomed over the battlefield, easy to see and—at more than 11 feet high (3.3m)—easy to shoot, the T-34 was less than 8 feet tall (2.4m) without the later cupola. It is 24 feet (7.3m) long, from the muzzle to the back of the track, and about 9½ feet (2.8m) wide. The tank weighs about 35 tons

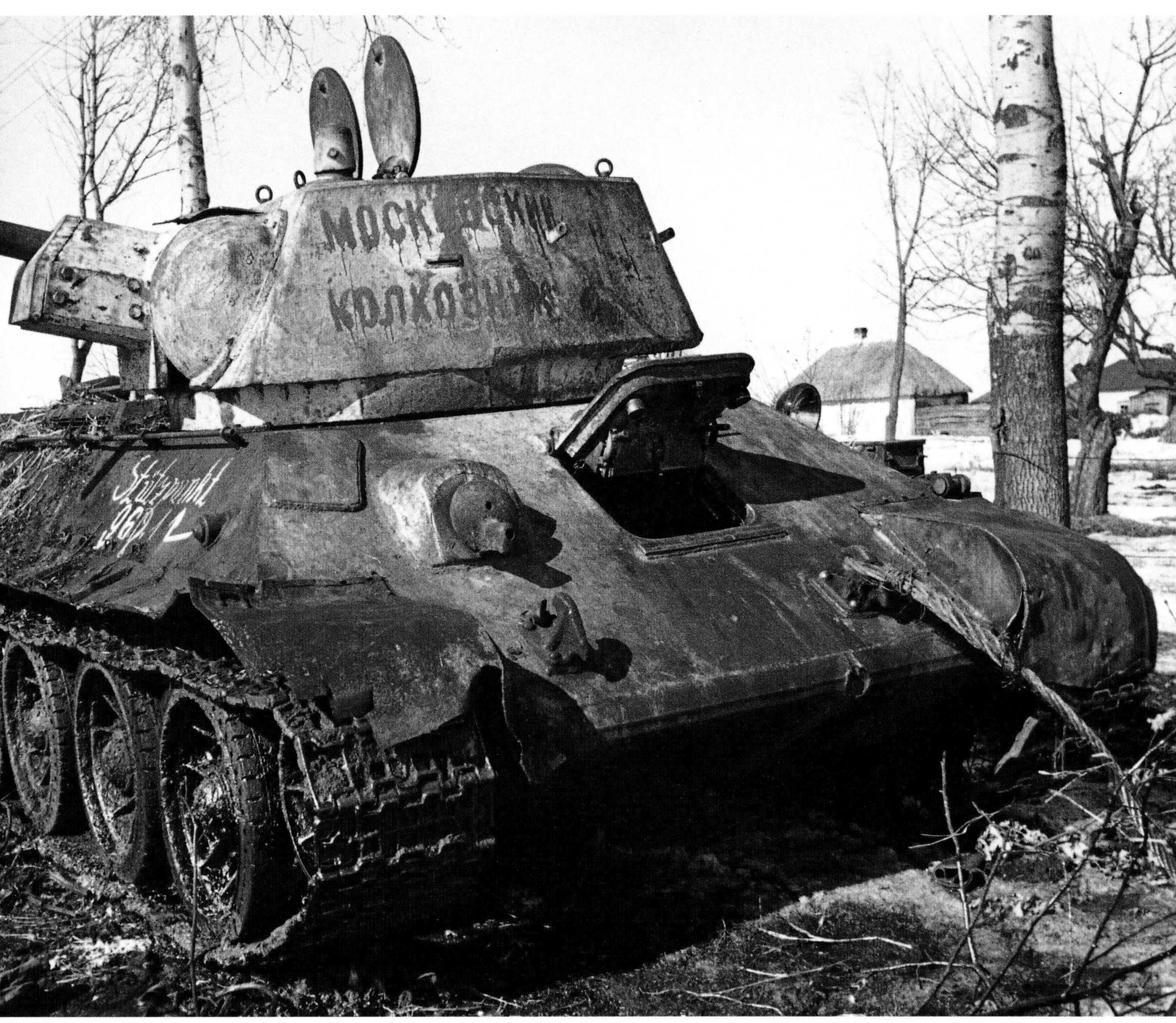

(31.7t) and exerts a ground pressure of just over 11 psi—light enough for excellent flotation over soft ground.

Primary armament is a long-barreled, high-velocity 85mm cannon, typically the Model 1944 Z1S L/51. Secondary weapons normally include two 7.62mm Model DT machine guns—one in a ball mount at the front of the tank, the other mounted co-axially with the main gun and operated by the gunner. A combat load of fifty-five main gun rounds are carried in bins under the turret, plus about three thousand rounds of linked 7.62mm ammo for the two machine guns.

Power for the tank comes from a massive 12-cylinder diesel engine, Model V-2-34. Water-cooled and rated to 500 hp at 1800 rpm, it gives the vehicle almost 16 hp per ton (0.9t). The T-34 is good for about 31 mph (49.8kph) on the road and has a basic range of 184 miles (296km).

CREW

The T-34 uses a crew of five: driver, bow gunner/assistant driver, loader, gunner, and commander. The driver

and bow gunner sit up front in the hull, much as their contemporaries in the American M4 Sherman.

Driving the T-34 is not for sissies. It is a notoriously brutal tank to drive at slow speeds. Steering is with lateral levers, the same as with most tanks of the World War II period, but the T-34's levers are stiff. As speed increases, the ride and controls smooth out, but the ideal driver for the tank is a guy who looks like a short linebacker. The compressed air cylinders, so handy for starting the engine on cold mornings, are on his left, along with a basic instrument panel.

But the driver has one great advantage: a hatch that opens forward for improved visibility and ventilation. While the rest of the crew is gagging on their own fumes and those of the engine and the guns, the driver is enjoying the breeze—at least until somebody fires on the tank.

On the right, the bow gunner waits patiently for enemy infantry to wander into his line of fire. Most Nazis figured out pretty early that this was a bad idea and stayed hidden until the T-34 had rumbled past before popping out of their holes to get off a flank shot with a Panzerfaust anti-tank weapon. The bow gunner didn't get a lot of business, but he did have several important functions. He often relieved the driver, letting him get some rest on long road marches. He helped with maintenance, housekeeping, guard duty, and all the other chores for a tank crew in the field. And when the driver or another member of the crew got killed, he could take over—a sort of onboard spare crew member.

An emergency escape hatch, often covered with hydraulic fluid from leaking seals, is mounted under the bow gunner's feet. Directly behind the driver, on the left side of the turret, is

OPPOSITE: **Jacques Littlefield's T-34 takes up a firing position, although the enemy surrendered fifty years ago.** **RIGHT, TOP:** **Tidy and spacious, the T-34's fighting compartment was far roomier than many of its World War II equivalents. The gunner's station and controls are on the left, the gun breech in the center.** **RIGHT, BOTTOM:** **Driver's station on the T-34. The controls are stiff and the instrumentation simple, but visibility is good and the tank is durable and reliable.**

the gunner's station, and his seat is attached to the side of the gun breech. He has a good sight, for that time, and fairly good visibility from his little overhead wide-field periscope. Turret drive is a combination electric/manual system—the gunner can use power to swing the gun into general alignment, then fine-tune the lay of the gun with the hand crank.

T-34 commanders also have their station on the left of the breech, with a seat right behind the gunner. The commander has a cupola with vision slots and periscopes. The slots are handy, except when enemy machine-gun and rifle fire is spattering against the turret. Then, bullet fragments are likely to spray inside and the TC risks injury by using the slots.

Another quirk of the T-34 is the loader's station—he's situated on the right side of the breech, and that means he serves the gun left-handed. It seems like a goofy way to do things, but it worked well enough just the same. T-34s did far more than their share of killing.

Rounds for the 85mm gun are stowed under the gun in bins and covered with neoprene mats. Since the turret doesn't use a basket or integral floor, these bins provide footing for the crew in the fighting compartment. There was a tendency in combat for the bins to be cluttered up with spent cases, inhibiting the loader's ability to dig out fresh ammunition, but this inconvenience didn't keep them from prevailing most of the time.

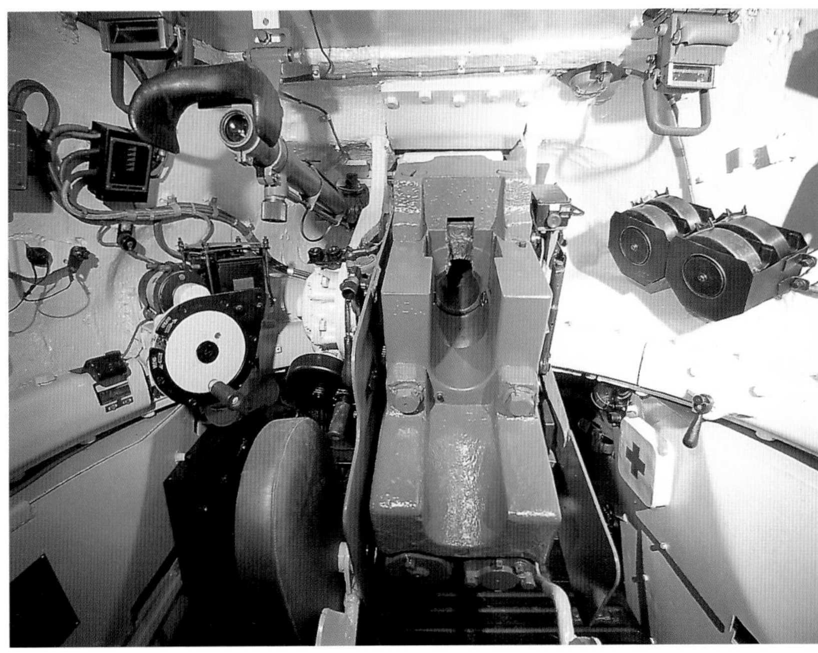

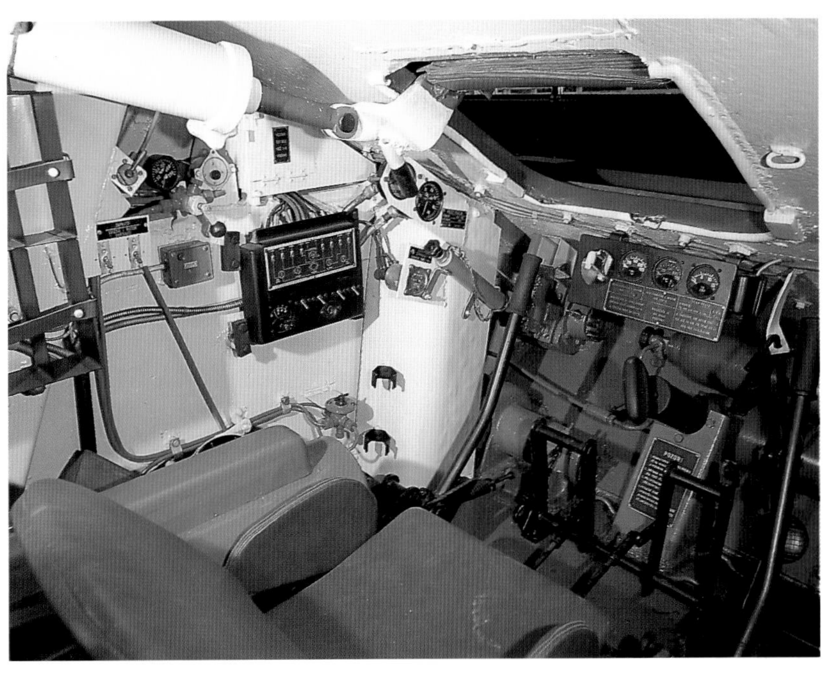

C H A P T E R S I X

THE M4 SHERMAN

The M4 Sherman Medium Tank was one of the most important, dominant, and successful weapon systems produced by any nation during all of World War II.

In a span of three years, nearly fifty thousand of them were built, in numerous variations and by many contractors. More Shermans were built than the combined total tank production of both Germany and England during the entire war. Shermans served with distinction in British, French, Russian, and American armored units during the war, and in many other nations in the years that followed. They've proved themselves in the most extreme climatic conditions, from the frigid Battle of the Bulge and frozen Chosin to the heat of the North African desert and Pacific jungle islands.

Despite that glowing success story, everybody who fought in them agreed that the Sherman was, in fact, a technologically mediocre tank. It had an inadequate gun, armor that wasn't quite thick enough, and a tall profile that seemed to say, "Here I am! Shoot me!" It had a cobbled-together design based on the foundation of an even more inadequate tank, the M3 Medium Tank (known as both the Lee and the Grant), from which it took its hull and power train.

Despite these deficiencies, the Sherman was a war winner. It earned its reputation by being competent, not excellent, and because it was available in huge numbers. They swarmed the battlefield, blasting away at German tanks that had better guns, thicker armor, and more experienced crews. While the German Tigers and Panthers might easily destroy a Sherman or two in a gunfight, there were always three or four others sneaking around behind for a shot at the enemy's vulnerable rear. John Whitehill, a WWII 4th Armored Division platoon and company commander, reports that in his unit, the SOP was for the whole platoon to gang up on one German tank. This intensity almost always caused the German tank to attempt escape. When it turned, exposing its tail end, one of the Shermans could usually destroy it.

While the M4 wasn't a wonder-weapon in any single area, it was fairly good in all its capabilities. Its 75mm gun couldn't inflict a puncture wound on a Tiger, but it could blow off a track. The effect of multiple hits on a Tiger turret or hull could still break things loose inside, start fires, and create casualties.

Although the Tiger's gun was clearly superior, unless the engine was running, the German crew had to hand-crank the turret around to engage. The Sherman crew, on the other hand, had a good, fast power traverse. That allowed the Sherman crew to be on target much faster and to get in four or five shots before the German tank fired its first round. The Sherman also had a gun stabilizer, which helped keep the gun on target while the tank was on the move, another edge in combat.

One other feature WWII Sherman crewmen still praise was the tank's remarkable reliability. As long as it was maintained—the fittings greased and the engine hand-cranked fifty times before a cold start—the M4 Sherman would fire right up in the morning and go all day, ranging freely over some pretty challenging terrain: up ravines and wadis, and through rivers, muck, and mire.

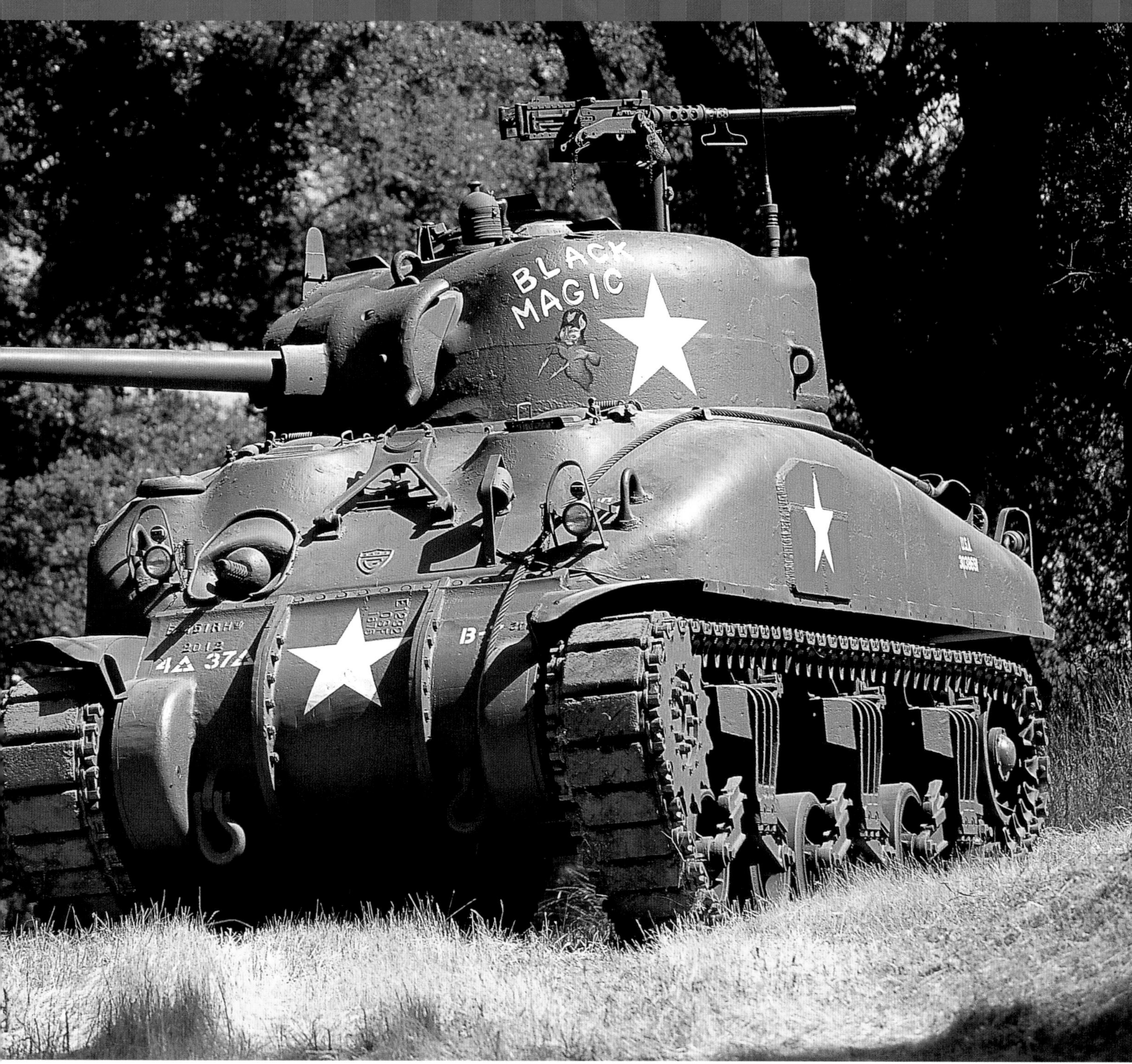

DESCRIPTION

The Sherman came in many shapes and sizes during and after World War II, and no one set of specifications is entirely accurate for the whole family. The M4A1 differed substantially from the M4A4, for example. Even within the model runs, the specs can vary depending on such variables as welded-on supplemental armor and other component parts.

The Sherman started out as a narrow, tall, light machine, measuring 8 feet 7 inches (2.6m) across and 11 feet 1 inch (3.3m) in height, and weighing in at 23 tons (20.8t). As the war progressed and the Sherman's design faults became (literally) painfully obvious, the tank gained

ABOVE: Certainly not the most advanced tank on the World War II battlefield but one of the most prolific, the M4 Sherman overwhelmed the Germans by weight of numbers, agility, and coordinated tactics. This beautiful example–a Canadian-built "Grizzly"–has been restored inside and out by Jacques Littlefield.

weight and bulk, picking up 4 inches (10.1cm) of side armor and an additional 8 tons (7.2t). Even so, it was lighter and more agile than most of the competition.

American armor units normally had gasoline-powered Shermans. Though their volatile fuel caught fire so easily that they were referred to as "Ronsons" (the lighter that was "guaranteed to light on the first try"), there was a good reason for using gas. American planners didn't want to have to supply two kinds of fuel to the front line (both diesel and gasoline). They had already standardized on gasoline for the support vehicles, so the tanks would use gasoline, too.

The use of the old M3 Lee hull and running gear wasn't a bad decision, and the basic design was modified during production to make it even better. The M4A1 combined a cast upper section with a welded lower hull as a foundation for the tank. The armor on the front glacis plate was 2 inches (5cm) thick and sloped between 37 and 55 degrees from vertical. The lower cast portion was also 2 inches (5cm) thick, sloped from 0 to 45 degrees. The sides of the hull were 1½ inches (3.8cm) thick, and the top surfaces had ½ to ¾ inches (1.2 to 1.9cm) of cast steel armor. The turret was cast, with 3 inches (7.6cm) of steel in front, 2 inches (5cm) on the sides and rear, and 1 inch (2.5cm) on the roof.

Many kinds of engines were used on Shermans over the years, but the A1—used by so many U.S. tankers—was propelled by a 9-cylinder air-cooled radial engine, a Continental R975, producing 350 hp at 2400 rpm. This engine, normally found in aircraft, used 80-octane gasoline, although similar radials used in M4s drank diesel.

The Sherman could negotiate a 60 percent grade, cross a trench up to 8 feet (2.4m) wide, and climb a 2-foot (61cm) wall. It could also ford a stream up to 40 inches (1m) deep without preparation. With lots of

OPPOSITE: America's not-so-secret weapon during World War II was production capacity. Here, M4A1 Sherman hull and power pack assemblies roll off the production line, ready for turret installation. **LEFT:** Mechanics install a turret in an M4 Sherman. Not all builders could cast the huge hull sections of the tank, and welded them up instead. These versions are designated simply M4 while the cast versions are M4A1. **BELOW:** The pilot model M4A1 on its birthday–June 9, 1942–poses proudly at Aberdeen Proving Ground, Maryland.

preparation, it could go swimming in the open ocean–where it could easily drown, crew and all, if conditions were not perfect. The British developed a canvas screen and framework–part of a large program of invention called "Hobart's funnies" after the general in charge of the effort–that provided just enough floatation for the Sherman. Some of these attempted to swim ashore at Normandy on D-day (June 6, 1944), and a few made it. Once ashore, the screens and frames were discarded and the tank was ready to move inland.

WEAPONRY

Over the years, there has been much wailing and gnashing of teeth about the Sherman's 75mm main gun. It was an anemic performer when new, and totally outclassed as an anti-tank weapon early in the war. While it worked against the German PzKpfw IIIs, it was less successful against the Mark IVs and a complete failure versus the Vs and VIs, whose front surface armor was impregnable to the M3 gun's slow round. Sherman crews overcame that by swarming opponents and attacking from the rear.

Tanks, however, used their guns for much more than fighting other tanks. In these alternate roles, the M3 gun excelled. This weapon was quite suitable for indirect fire missions–i.e., artillery assignments–in ways that the German guns couldn't emulate. U.S. gunners could lob HE rounds over ridges and hills on top of

ABOVE: Fred Popkey's handsome M4 was featured in James Garner's feature film *Tank*, and regularly appears during reenactment displays in the Washington, D.C., area. **LEFT:** Many Shermans used the fabled "Ma Duce" .50cal heavy machine gun for secondary armament. Accurate to a mile (1.6km), and deadly against light vehicles, aircraft, and troops in the open, Ma Duce was–and still is–a fearsome weapon. **OPPOSITE:** An M4 Sherman crew loads up for a day of training, sometime before shipping out for overseas.

enemy assembly areas. They could create havoc among enemy soldiers by destroying vehicles that enemy commanders thought were safe from tank fire.

This indirect fire capability made the Sherman extremely valuable in a wide variety of situations. Indirect fire was a reliable way of reducing pillboxes, enemy gun positions, resupply points, troop concentrations, vehicle parks, convoys, bunkers, and bridges. It also allowed the Sherman to fire illumination rounds for night observation and combat. These were things a high-velocity anti-tank gun did poorly—or not at all.

Besides the 75mm cannon, the Sherman typically mounted two or three machine guns, a .50cal M2 heavy-barreled machine gun behind the TC's hatch—useful against thin-skinned vehicles or troops at long range—plus at least one M1919A4 .30cal for use against airplanes and anything else within 500 yards (457.2m).

FIRE CONTROL

Sherman gunners were the key crew members, the foundation of the tank's mission. Consequently, the gunner's station was equipped with excellent systems for acquiring and engaging targets. For direct fire within a mile (1.6km)—the system's maximum range against tanks—the gunner used an M4 periscope, with its small integral M38 telescopic sight, for general lay of the gun, then switched to the M55 telescopic sight for precision lay.

For indirect fire (a feature common in all U.S. tanks until the M1 Abrams) the gunner had an M19 Azimuth Indicator, a Gunner's Quadrant M1, and an Elevation Quadrant M9. These devices were used with field artillery and allowed precise fire against unseen targets—with the help, of course, of a forward observer reporting back by radio or land line.

AMMUNITION

Since the Sherman and its 75mm gun were in such widespread use, and since there were many complaints about the gun's ability to puncture enemy armor, a wide variety of ammunition was available for it. These included APC, AP, HE (with and without a supercharge propellant load), and HC (a white phosphorus smoke round). Of these, the APC and AP rounds were most commonly used in World War II. At 1,000 yards (914.4m), the APC round would punch through just 2⅛ inches (5.5cm) of homogenous steel armor tilted at 30 degrees. The AP was good for just 2 inches (5cm).

An experimental high-velocity AP round was developed and tested. It penetrated to almost 4 inches (10.1cm), but wasn't issued—much to the disgust and dismay of many Sherman crews.

The Sherman's standard anti-tank rounds were pretty slow when compared to the competition—about 2,000 fps (609.6mps)—but the experimental round was pumped up to 2,800 fps (853.4mps). Maximum range for both the APC and HE (supercharged) rounds was 14,000 yards (12,801.6km) (just

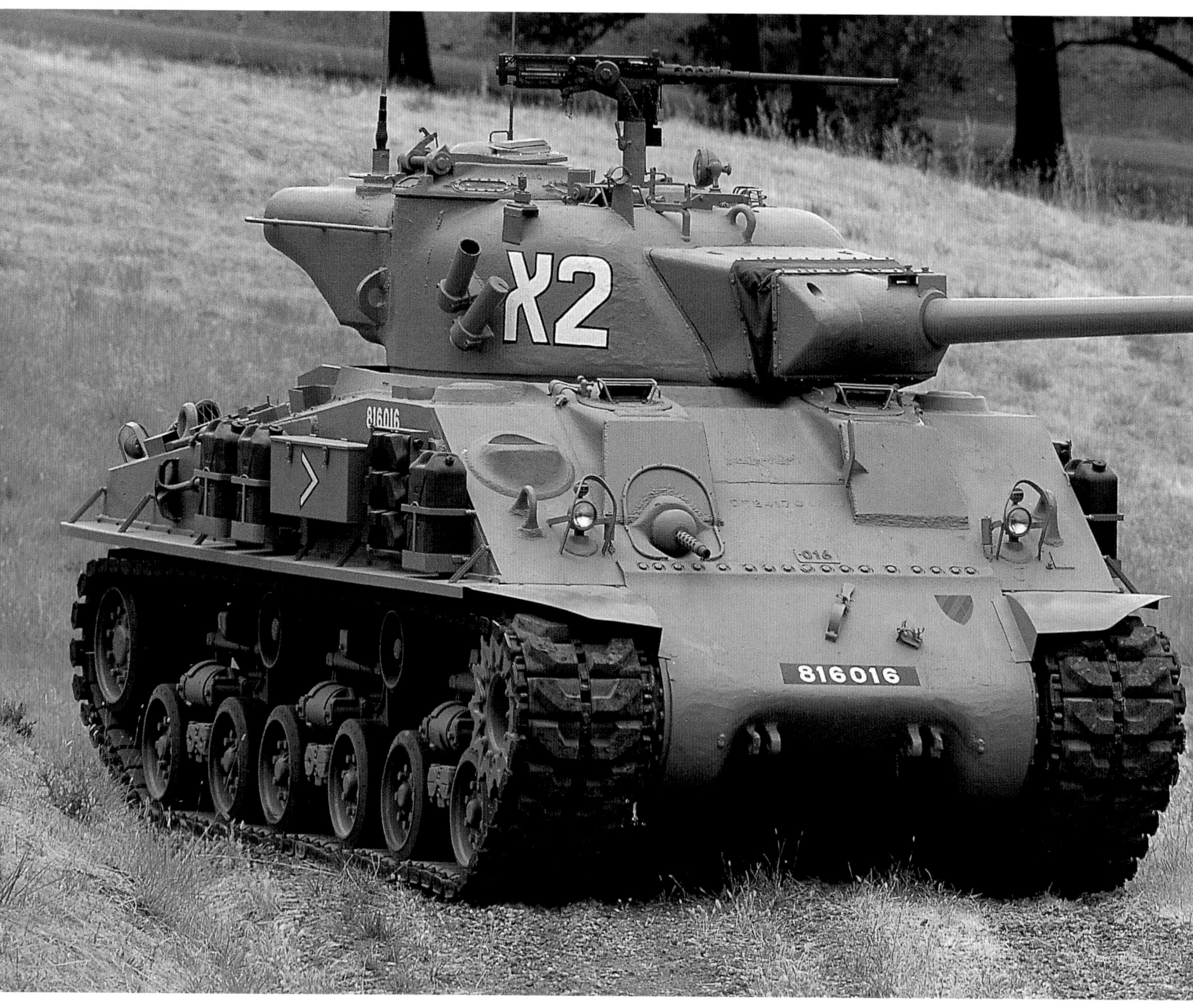

shy of 8 miles [12.8km]). Maximum rate of fire on the main gun was twenty rounds per minute.

The 76mm round used on some M4s was a substantial improvement. Although the projectile's girth was just a millimeter bigger, the propellant capacity of the case was about 50 percent greater than that of the 75mm version. A longer barrel allowed more propellant energy to act on the projectile, producing better penetration data—but still not good enough to beat a Tiger head on.

CREW

The Sherman needed a five-man crew: driver, bow machine gunner, loader, gunner, and commander. The driver and bow machine gunner worked in the front of the hull while the other three inhabited the turret, with the TC on the right rear, the gunner on the right front, and the loader on the left of the gun.

The driver sits at the left front of the tank in a fairly spacious compartment. On his immediate right is the big transmission housing, with the bow gunner sitting on the far right. Both have hatches with M6 periscopes for observing to the front

LEFT: This M50 Super Sherman (from Jacques Littlefield's collection) shows the scars of close-quarter combat from its years with the Israeli Army. The gun is a French copy of the German high-velocity 75mm cannon used in the Panther. RIGHT: Gunner's station, Super Sherman tank.

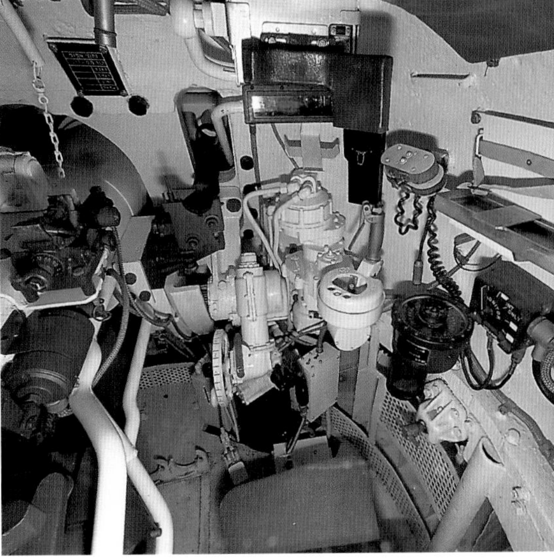

while buttoned up. The periscopes are normally retracted to keep them clean and undamaged. They are simply pushed up for use.

An instrument panel on the driver's left indicates rpm, oil and water temperature, and fuel quantity for each tank. There is also an ammeter, warning lights for low oil pressure and fire, the vehicle's circuit breakers, light switches, and the control for the tank's siren. On the lower right of the panel are the two magneto switches and the starter switch. Next to the panel is the driver's compass. Early Shermans also got a fuel dilution control and a priming pump switch on the panel.

Steering is done with lateral levers, each braking a track. Pulling back on both levers stops the tank. A hand throttle to the right of the laterals allows the driver to set a high rpm for battery charging or warm-up. Driving is done with a conventional accelerator pedal on the deck.

The Sherman driver shifts gears manually with a shift control on his right. His transmission is a synchromesh 5-speed, with one reverse gear. On a good road, he can drive the M4A1 about 120 miles (193km) on a 175-gallon (662.3L) tank of gas–about .7 miles (1.1km) to the gallon (3.7L). He can putter along at up to 21 mph (33.7kph) in fifth gear.

The specifications say you could accelerate up to 24 mph (38.6kph) for brief periods, perhaps to pass. With the 450 hp Ford V-8 water-cooled engine, the M4A3 can cruise down the road at 26 mph (41.8kph) (official figure) or 40 mph (64.3kph) (with the governor "adjusted," according to ex-crewmen).

The bow machine gunner/assistant driver sits on the far side of the transmission, often asleep. He really doesn't have much to do most of the time, unless the driver gets killed. He has a machine gun but can aim it only by watching his tracers. Even so, he is a valuable member of the crew, and in cold weather the other members rotated positions in order to get his seat–the only warm spot in the tank. He and the driver generally traded positions on long road marches to keep the driver fresh and awake. Under very stressful conditions, all crew members rotated to the position, allowing all to sleep in turn.

Both the driver and the assistant could, if necessary, worm their way back into the turret through openings in the turret basket. Sometimes they got dragged out of their seats through the turret after the Sherman took a hit on the front surfaces and one or both were injured. It was a difficult maneuver, but one that many tank crews performed under fire.

The gunner sits on the right front of the turret, below the TC's level. Isolated from the outside world except for his periscope and sights, the gunner has a power traverse to rapidly bring the gun to bear, and hand controls for the final accurate lay. Foot switches on the deck fire the gun or the co-ax.

There were always problems with the Sherman's sight systems—and many options were tried. The standard gunner's M4 periscope had a small, low-power M38A1 telescope incorporated on the right side of the viewer, and it could be used to engage targets. This viewing system was connected to the gun by a linkage system that had to be carefully—and frequently—adjusted. Crews proposed adding a fixed telescopic sight. For this, the gun mount design had to be modified, and the M55 sight was the result.

Still, when the Sherman's sight system works properly and the gunner knows his business, they can be extremely effective. Some gunners defeated Panthers by bouncing an AP round off the bottom of the enemy's mantlet, and down into the thin roof armor over the driver's compartment. That feat required a good, accurate gun—and a cool, courageous gunner.

The commander sits or stands on the right rear of the turret, searching for targets, working the radio, inspecting the maps, and exhorting the crew on the intercom.

The loader gets the left side of the turret to himself, but since he has to flip 20-pound (9kg) main gun rounds around and keep the co-ax ammunition box full, it's just as well he has that space. The loader sometimes is also responsible for operating the radios in the rear of the turret, although the TC often assumed this responsibility. On many tanks the loader is responsible for a smoke bomb mortar. This device, a British invention, would eject a 2-inch (5cm) grenade 35 to 150 yards (32 to 137.1m) in front of the tank and, after a short interval, produce a thick cloud of white smoke to cover a quick getaway.

OPPOSITE: Sherman tanks of the French forces line the streets of Marburg, Germany, on April 26, 1951. The Sherman served for many years and in many armies after World War II.

SPECIFICATIONS	**Medium Tank M4A1**
Crew	5
Weight	66,800 lbs (30.3t) (combat loaded)
Length with gun forward	230 in (5.8m)
Turret height	108 in (2.7m)
Width	103 in (261.6cm)
Ground clearance	17 in (43.1cm)
Ground pressure	13.7 lbs (6.2kg)
Propulsion	Continental R975 radial, air-cooled engine, 9 cylinders, displacing 973 cubic inches; 400 hp (gross) at 2400 rpm
Transmission	Synchromesh; five forward, one reverse gear
Speed	21 mph (33.7kph) on road, max
Range	120 miles (193km)
Obstacle crossing	Vertical: 24 in (61cm) Trench: 7.5 ft (2.2m)
Main armament	75mm Gun M3 in Mount M334
Co-axial weapon	.30cal M1919A4
Loader's weapon	none
Commander's weapon	.50cal M2 with heavy barrel in flex mount on turret roof
NBC protection	none

VULCAIN
A
817 258

LEFT: A Sherman crewman uses the .50cal Ma Duce against German positions guarding the Marne River bridge.

COMBAT HISTORY

As with the M3 and M5 Stuart, the American Sherman first went to war wearing British colors. The first production tanks were stripped from U.S. Army units, even before American tank crews could be trained in them, and shipped to British forces in North Africa. This was an emergency response to a rampaging Afrika Korps, the loss of Tobruk, and the threatened loss of Egypt and the whole Mediterranean to the Axis.

Three hundred and eighteen M4A1s and A2s arrived in early September 1942. They were hastily converted to British 8th Army standards, and sent to battle five weeks later at El Alamein. It was not an auspicious baptism.

A force of Panzer IIIs and IVs, with excellent 50mm and 75mm cannon, engaged units of the British 2nd Armoured Brigade about sunrise on October 23, 1942. Fire was exchanged at long range, about 2,000 yards (1,828.8m), well beyond normal effective ranges for either force. A few tanks were hit and caught fire on both sides; then the Germans withdrew. It was first blood for the Sherman, and the beginning of a long combat history.

The Sherman soon became the most common medium tank in British service, with more than 15,000 supplied by the end of the war. U.S. armor units soon joined the Brits in November 1942 with landings around Casablanca and Oran.

There was a lot to learn about the new tank and the new war. The very first U.S. Shermans to see combat, a platoon of five attached to 2nd Battalion, 13th Armored Regiment, were all destroyed in action near Tebourba on December 6, 1942. Shermans from 2nd and 3rd Battalions, 1st Armored Regiment, were annihilated in fighting around the Faid Pass in February 1943. Things would get better soon, however. Even though many thousands more would be lost in the years to follow, the Shermans would destroy even more German and Italian tanks in return.

Shermans in American service fought eastward across North Africa, then on to Sicily, up the muddy boot of Italy. They came ashore by the thousands on the Normandy coast in June 1944 and fought for weeks in the Bocage country behind the invasion beaches. Then Shermans from General George Patton's 4th Armored Division broke out and began a race across France, closely chasing a German army in retreat. The Germans counterattacked in December, in the deep woods around Bastogne, Belgium, and nearly defeated the overextended and complacent Allied forces before their own fuel and ammunition ran out.

In the Pacific, the M4 Sherman debuted in November 1943 at

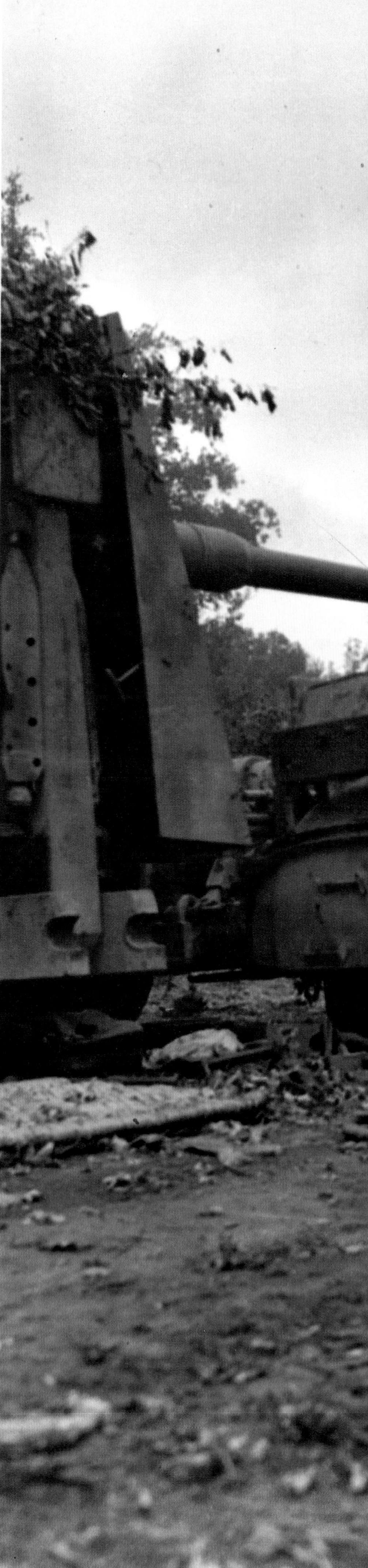

RIGHT: A M4A1 blasts past a knocked-out German 88. The Sherman has the Culin hedgerow cutter still installed and a stack of sandbags to augment the inadequate front slope armor. **BELOW:** An Army tank mechanic works on the 75mm gun. Even when knocked out in combat, Shermans were frequently repaired and sent back into action, complete with bloodstains and a new crew.

"Terrible" Tarawa, where a botched amphibious assault put Marines and tanks into the surf hundreds of yards offshore, with disastrous consequences. But the Sherman performed so well at reducing Japanese gun positions and emplacements that the Marine commander, Major General Holland M. "Howling Mad" Smith, asked that the Shermans–and not the light M5 Stuarts–be used in future beach assaults.

And so they were: at Cape Gloucester, New Britain, Bougainville, Biak, Kwajalein, up the long Philippine chain, and on to Tinian, Iwo Jima, and Okinawa. While many were lost to land mines, 47mm anti-tank guns, and even suicidal Japanese infantry, Shermans were a valuable member of the Pacific combat team.

After the war, the M4 Sherman continued to serve the U.S. Army and a large number of other nations, and went to war again in Korea in 1950. Some would go on to Israel, where the Sherman has had a long and successful combat career, only recently being retired from service.

192762

CHAPTER SEVEN

GERMANY'S PANZERKAMPFWAGEN

PZKPFW V PANTHER

The origins of the Panzerkampfwagen V Panther go back to the combat debut of the Russian T-34/76 in October 1941. Until that moment, the Panzer IV pretty well ruled the battlefield, annihilating Soviet defenders. German tankers and their leaders were confident of their vehicles, tactics, weapons, and objectives; then the T-34 changed everything. As a design, it was momentarily invincible. Only the incompetence of the Russian commanders and staff kept it from winning the war on the eastern front then and there.

While still on the drawing board, the Mark V came close to being a T-34 clone, but that proposal was rejected for several reasons. For one, casualties from friendly fire would be inevitable. For another, Germany didn't have aluminum to spare for the T-34's excellent diesel engine. Finally, German planners just could not accept the kind of technological defeat that such a decision would represent. They would not duplicate—they would surpass.

The mature Panther (it went through many changes) is, even so, essentially a T-34 in drag—with each of the original's distinctive features emphasized to the extreme. Its protective armor is quite thick—nearly 5 inches (12.7cm) on the front surfaces—and is well sloped all around. Its gun is a very long-barreled high-velocity 75mm cannon. After some teething problems, its drivetrain became a reliable, powerful system allowing great mobility. It is a low tank, with excellent visibility for the TC from within an armored cupola.

One of the best features of the Panther was that 75mm gun, in its final long-barreled form. Lots of tanks and tank destroyers used a 75mm gun, but the Panther's was of an improved design. A much longer tube and an improved propellant significantly pumped up the projectile's velocity. That allowed a Panther crew to engage U.S., British, and Russian tanks at ranges of more than 1,000 yards (914.4m), well beyond the

ABOVE: This Panther has taken multiple hits on its sturdy glacis plate and has finally succumbed. It is a second-generation model. LEFT: The British Tank Museum at Bovington displays this fine specimen of the Panther breed, a late G model with "ambush" paint scheme. OPPOSITE: An early model Panther, the first generation D, captured in Italy.

ability of the Shermans and T-34s to effectively reply. Armor historian Mike Kendall states, "During World War II, the German arms manufacturers were technically the best in the world in workmanship and design. This technical superiority plus a quality workforce helped make the German guns the best in the war."

Even though more than five thousand PzKpfw V Panthers were built during World War II, it was not enough to fight off the closing ring of fire from Shermans and T-34s. By the time production Panthers rolled onto the battlefield, the Allies had already beaten the Axis in the great production race, and the best that could be done was postpone defeat.

Sometimes, particularly in Normandy before the breakout, the only practical way to deal with Panthers was with very big guns, such as large naval rifles with bores from 5 to 16 inches (12.7 to 40.6cm) in diameter. Naval gunfire support decimated many Panzer divisions. The Panzer Lehr Division lost half its tanks and took three days to recover from a single bombardment in June 1944. In Sicily and Italy, field artillery took on the big cats when nothing else would work. A close miss, within 10 or 20 yards (9.1 or 18.2m), by an 8-inch (20.3cm) HE round could flip a Panther upside down. Anything closer could rip it apart.

The most practical and efficient way to destroy German tanks was by

air attack. British pilots flying Typhoons, Americans in P-47 Thunderbolts, and Russians in Il-2s and P-39s formed squadrons dedicated to ground attack missions. Four-inch (10.1cm) rocket fire and 20mm cannon projectiles ripped open Panthers through their thin top armor and detonated their main gun rounds in the ready racks. The resulting internal explosions typically ripped the tanks apart at the seams.

Even so, the Panther was certainly one of the best tanks of the war, if not the best, as a complete package of firepower, mobility, and protection.

ABOVE: Tired tank, tired commander, somewhere in Italy, 1944. RIGHT: The Tiger tank, like this one on the move in Italy sometime in 1944, totally intimidated Allied forces. It was largely invulnerable to any single weapon available, except at the top and rear of the vehicle. OPPOSITE: A massive Tiger I pauses in Russia while the infantry slog past.

PZKPFW VI: TIGER

Certainly the most feared tanks of the later war years were the German Tigers. There were two versions, the early Tiger and the huge, heavy Königstiger, or "King Tiger." It was the King Tiger especially that frightened its enemies, and with good reason.

Although only about fifteen hundred were ever built, and only seven are known to survive outside Russia, the German PzKpfw VI Tiger WWII heavy tank had a profound effect on the land war in Europe and on tank design in the years that followed. The Tiger combined the huge, accurate, extremely effective, and legendary 88mm gun with a very heavily armored hull and turret, a combination that could outrange and outfight virtually any other tank it encountered. An M4A3 Sherman couldn't penetrate the armor on the front of a Tiger from even point-blank range—but the Tiger could take the Sherman out, face to face, at a range of 2 miles (3.2km). It was one of those designs that could have changed the course of the war if it had been used earlier and better. Fortunately for the Allies, its capabilities were squandered and the great Tigers were killed off, one by one.

German tank divisions were built around two kinds of tanks, one heavy and one light. In the war's early years, these were the Mark III and Mark IV. The III, however, didn't do as well as expected against the British Matilda–and didn't do well at all against the Russian T-34/76–so, in 1941, a design program for a new, dominant heavy tank, based around the 88mm gun, was initiated.

The result was large and heavy, and designed for simplified production.

It was a bit underpowered at first, and there were some drivetrain problems with many of the early examples. It was never intended to be used as a conventional MBT, but rather for use in specialized battalions of thirty Tigers each, under the tactical control of corps or army headquarters, at critical locations where shock value was important.

PZKPFW VI MARK I

The first Tigers had, in many respects, a design separate from that of the later Mark IIs, the King Tiger. These early versions were designed for rapid construction and were simpler than the Mark IIs. Much of the Mark I was thick, flat sheet-steel plate, with minimal slope.

The basic Tiger Mark I was 27 feet (8.2m) long, 12 feet (3.6m) wide, and more than 9 feet (2.7m) high. It weighed a staggering 121,235 pounds (55,040.6kg)—more than 60 tons (54.4t). It was too wide for many roads and too heavy for many bridges. The Tiger was even too wide to transport by rail without replacing the tracks with temporary narrow versions. All this naturally restricted the tank's mobility.

The Tiger's hide was extremely thick and tough, with up to 4.33 inches (11cm) on the gun mantlet and almost 4 inches (10.1cm) on the glacis plate. At the thinnest point, the armor was still more than an inch (2.5cm) thick. Generally, it was impervious to main tank rounds from almost everything on the battlefield—except, that is, from the British 17-pounder (7.7kg) with its high-velocity sabot round.

PZKPFW VI MARK II

The next Tiger upgrade, the Mark II or King Tiger, had well-sloped armor and other variations that made it extremely effective in solo engagements. Fewer than five hundred were built, though, and many were lost due to breakdowns, fuel shortages, and from the heavy tank's inability to keep up with fast-moving battles.

Both the Tiger I and Tiger II used an 88mm gun, but with variations. The

OPPOSITE: A rare surviving Tiger I tank on display at Aberdeen Proving Ground, Maryland.
RIGHT: The Tiger II was really an entirely new tank in many ways, particularly the well-shaped turret.
BELOW: The German Army Tank Museum at Munster exhibits this handsome Tiger II, originally captured by American forces at the Battle of the Bulge and later returned for display.

King Tiger used a long-barreled version that could outshoot any tank on the battlefield. That 88mm gun is the same weapon that shocked and dismayed U.S. and British tankers in the North African desert. Originally designed as an anti-aircraft weapon, its ability to depress to the horizontal, its extreme range, and its heavy caliber all combined to make it highly successful against Allied armor. The 88 could easily outrange Allied tanks, destroying them at ranges where reply was impossible. The King Tiger's 88 had a longer barrel, fired a "hotter" round with far more propellant, and threw a projectile with greater velocity than the Tiger I's.

As part of the development program for the Tiger, the Germans assembled ballistic comparison tables for the new tank and its principal expected opponents. The data was impressive. The Tiger II (the basic production version) could reliably kill a Cromwell, Churchill, Sherman, or T-34 with a turret hit at about 2 miles (3.2km). None of these tanks could kill a Tiger with a similar hit at any range, including point-blank. The Sherman's 75mm gun could theoretically achieve penetration on the hull sides at about 100 yards (91.4m), but not on the hull, turret rear, or anywhere else. The Sherman's 76mm gun performed a bit better, with penetration on the turret sides at just over 1,000 yards (914.4m) and the hull at 1,700 yards (1,554.4m), but even that gun had to be within 375 yards (342.9m) for a shot at the Tiger's tail. Again, only the British 17-pounder (7.7kg) and special ammunition had a prayer of killing the Tiger head-on, and then at ranges of 1,000 yards (914.4m)—about half the effective range of the Tiger's own gun.

Although the Tiger I had been boxy and slab-sided, the general design and layout of the Tiger II tank was, despite its bulk and weight, excellent. The turret was large, slender, and difficult to hit except from the side. The thick armor on the King Tiger was well sloped. The commander had good visibility from his cupola at the rear. The massive ammunition rounds were stowed in racks easily accessible for the loader. Despite the

RIGHT: Another rare surviving Tiger II, this one in Belgium.

BELOW: Early in the Battle of the Bulge, in December 1944, German forces made a desperate drive out of the Ardennes forest before their fuel and ammunition ran out. This Tiger II rumbles past cold, miserable, captured American soldiers early in the campaign, while there was still hope it would succeed.

weight of the vehicle, the Tiger's steering system made it easier to drive than most of its contemporaries.

Power for the Tiger came from a 700-hp Maybach HL230 P45 V-12 gasoline engine driving an 8-speed preselect transmission. Although the Tiger's reputation was one of ponderous, slow movement, its mobility was actually about the same as lighter tanks—25 mph (40.2kph) on the road, and about half that across-country. An excellent torsion-bar suspension and eight road wheels to a side made for a smooth, comfortable ride. Fuel economy was understandably poor. As a result, the range of the Tiger was only 62 road miles (99.7km)—another shortcoming.

Despite its excellent design characteristics, the Tiger wasn't fully successful, and was phased out starting in the summer of 1944. On the frigid eastern front, its tracks froze to the ground if the vehicle remained immobile for too long. The Tiger crews used grenades to loosen the tracks before they could again move the tank. This made them vulnerable to surprise attack. The Russians timed their attacks for dawn or before, in part to capitalize on this defect.

Even in good weather, the Tiger sometimes had catastrophic mobility problems. The first production tanks were rushed, at Hitler's assistance, to the eastern front for the 1942 siege of Leningrad. Hitler's impatience meant crews went untrained and the brand-new vehicles' teething problems went uncorrected. The Tigers broke down on the road or bogged down in soft terrain, and platoons of them were lost.

Still, attacking from ambush, the Tiger could ravage Allied armor. During the breakout after the Normandy invasion, a single Tiger destroyed twenty-five tanks in one engagement, halting the advance of an entire U.S. division before it, too, was destroyed.

THE SOVIET T-55

The Russian T-55 is, in one way at least, the most successful tank ever built. It is, without a doubt, the most prolific armored vehicle, with about 100,000 built, in dozens of variants and Chinese copies, for dozens of nations. It has been, along with many other Russian weapon systems, an export success story of classic proportions.

The T-55 is still found in the front rank of the armor formations of many nations, even though its roots go back to 1944 and a Soviet medium tank called the T-44. The T-44 evolved into the T-54, the first of which appeared in 1946, and set the standard for Soviet tank design with a sleek, low turret that was calculated to shed anti-tank rounds with ease. The T-54, in turn, was upgraded again into its final, classic form, the T-55, a virtually identical vehicle, but with additional ammunition storage and a new, improved gun. This new version of the 100mm gun had a longer barrel, producing higher muzzle velocity.

CREW

The T-55 has a crew of four, with the driver up front and the TC, gunner, and loader in the fighting compartment. The driver controls the vehicle with "laterals" and views the terrain ahead during combat through two periscopes. One periscope can be replaced by a TVN-2 IR periscope for night operations in conjunction with the IR searchlight on the turret.

A major problem for TCs at the time the T-55 was developed was vision during battle. Most T-55 commanders prefer to stand exposed in the hatch, risking sniper fire, artillery rounds, and other hazards of the bat-

LEFT: Captain V. Karanov, a tank company commander, uses a flag signal to convey orders to his unit. RIGHT: Here comes the Red Horde, right out of the nightmares of NATO planners. The tanks are T-55s–obsolete today but still in service around the world, and very modern back in the 1960s and 1970s, when they were the mainstay of Soviet land forces.

345
345
340

tlefield, rather than be dependent on a couple of feeble vision blocks or a tiny periscope to identify and engage the enemy. The T-55 includes a cupola for the TC, with 360-degree rotation. Two periscopes in the cupola roof provide a superior view of the battlefield. The commander has a TPK-1 sight to engage the target, or he can hand it off to the gunner.

The gunner sits in front of and below the TC. His TSh 2-22 sight provides either 3.5X or 7X magnification. He typically uses the low power to acquire the target, then switches to higher magnification for precise aiming.

The loader on the T-55 is preferably a left-hander. He works from the right side of the gun and has to ram rounds into the breech with his left hand and arm, a very awkward move for right-handed people.

DESCRIPTION

The hull of the T-55 is welded, rolled-plate armor. The armor is nearly 4 inches (10.1cm) thick at the front glacis plate and angled at 60 degrees. This angle doubles its effective protection. There is just over 3 inches (7.6cm) of armor on the upper hull sides and only ¾ inch (1.9cm) on the lower hull sides, behind the road wheels. The turret front is a solid 8 inches (20.3cm) of cast steel, thinning out to about 6 inches (15.2cm) on the turret sides and only 2½ inches (6.3.cm) at the rear. The turret roof is 1½ inches (3.8cm) thick, enough to shed artillery splinters and some cannon fire from ground attack aircraft—but not enough to protect against aerial anti-tank rockets, a lucky direct hit from an artillery round, or a rocket-propelled grenade (RPG) launched from an overhead position.

T-55s are most often equipped with the D-10T gun, a 100mm rifled weapon based on the WWII design used in the successful SU-100. Early

OPPOSITE: This happy quartet have just climbed down from their T-55 to pose for the photographer from TASS. They will probably have to ford this river using a snorkel attachment that will allow the tank to crawl along the river bottom, and then they won't be smiling. BELOW: A column of T-55s rumble down a well-used tank trail in the Leningrad Military District.

models lacked stabilization and power traverse and elevation, but that changed with the A model, introduced in 1951. The gun can still be elevated and traversed by hand, but it is a slow process, only intended for emergency use. The power traverse system rotates the turret in twenty-one seconds.

Full elevation for the main gun is +18 degrees. It will depress to -5 degrees, with stabilization for the vertical and horizontal planes. Range finding is done with a stadiametric system.

The D-10T fires HE fragmentation, AP, HE anti-tank, and sabot rounds, with muzzle velocities ranging from 2,953 to 4,692 fps (900 to 1,430mps), depending on the round. Typical rate of fire is four rounds per minute. Early T-55s lacked a bore evacuator, and the turret filled up with noxious fumes every time the gun fired, endangering the crew. That led to another early modification, a bore evacuator, introduced along with gun stabilization, in the A model. (Today, despite the T-55's age and its well-worn guns, there is enough of a market for the system's 100mm ammunition that a Belgian company, Mecar, has developed a new line of rounds specifically for the D-10T and its variants.) Forty-three rounds of ammunition are carried for the main gun, plus thirty-five hundred rounds for the 7.62mm machine guns.

The engine is mounted transversely at the rear of the hull, and can be started electrically or from a compressed air cylinder—an ingenious and reliable method for starting anytime, particularly in extreme cold weather. The tank is refilled via an onboard AK-150 compressor (unlike the earlier T-34, which had to be recharged from an external source of compressed air).

It is a rough tank to drive, according to the drivers. Those best at it are short and very strong.

Like much Soviet armor, it is simple, basic, reliable, economical, and easily produced. It burns oil, even when the engine is new, and smokes more than comparable Western vehicles. The Soviets didn't care. They had plenty of oil, plus a reservoir on the deck of the hull to replenish all the oil the engine could burn. There is an important, and often overlooked, aspect to the T-55 and other Russian designs: the engines start easily in any weather, and keep running. The tanks get where they're going and arrive ready to fight. Sure, the crew feels tired and beat up, but crew comfort was never a major selling point with Russian armor—or anybody else's, for that matter.

It is a fighting machine, designed to dominate the battlefield of the 1950s. In its sometimes coarse way, the T-55 has elements of genius and

elegance inherent in its design philosophy, its shape and subsystems. It has a low-profile, bulletproof design, a great gun for its time, plenty of power, and a good drivetrain—all of the fundamentals of armor in one handsome package.

Thousands of T-55 tanks still serve Cuba, Russia, North Korea, Egypt, Syria, and many other nations. Even Iraq has a few left after the Gulf War, though not many. With the global draw-down of forces, the T-55 is being discarded by the Russians and some other nations, sold for scrap or to collectors.

RIGHT: The T-55 helped pioneer night vision technology with its infrared searchlight (visible on the left of the gun). This standard model is followed by a MT-55 bridge-layer, an essential vehicle for operations in the well-watered battlefields of Germany and France.

Today, a T-55 can be bought for about $10,000. Quite a few are in the hands of American and British private collectors. Getting parts is sometimes difficult but not impossible. Ammunition is another story. The weapons have been "de-milled" and can't be fired, although they are generally cosmetically correct.

SPECIFICATIONS	T-55
Crew	4
Weight	80,000 lbs (36.3t)
Length with gun forward	29 ft (8.8m)
Turret height	7 ft ¾ in (2.15m)
Width	10 ft ¾ in (3.27m)
Ground clearance	16¼ in (42.5cm)
Ground pressure	1,149 lbs (521.6kg)
Propulsion	580 hp V-12 diesel model V-55
Transmission	Manual; five forward, one reverse gear
Speed	31 mph (49.8kph)
Acceleration	not available
Range	375 miles (603.3km) with aux. tanks
Obstacle crossing	Vertical: .8m Trench: 2.7m
Main armament	100mm
Co-axial weapon	7.62mm
Loader's weapon	7.62mm
Commander's weapon	12.7mm
NBC protection	Starting with the T-55A model in 1963

822
822

CHAPTER NINE

THE M551 SHERIDAN

The M551 Sheridan is a light tank in the grand tradition—compact, quick, and, except for its stealth and speed, without much protection. It carries a huge M81 152mm main gun and missile launcher, originally intended to defeat enemy tanks at long range. In actual combat, though, the gun fires primarily canister rounds—ten thousand steel darts emerging from the tube red-hot, streaking downrange, cutting down anything and anybody across a wide swath. The first time the Sheridan fired the 152mm gun in Vietnam, eighty-two enemy bodies littered the battlefield.

The Sheridan has had a troubled but active career. For the past decade or so, it has been the only U.S. armor available for airborne assaults conducted by the legendary 82nd Airborne Division or its parent, XVIII Airborne Corps, based at Fort Bragg, North Carolina.

Originally christened the Armored Reconnaissance/Airborne Assault Vehicle M551, the Sheridan was developed in the early 1960s and produced in the latter part of the decade. About the time the vehicles were coming off the production line in volume, somebody discovered they were lemons. A national scandal ensued. Congressional hearings were held. The Sheridan was stored while major problems with the gun and the automotive system were resolved. The M551 was issued for just a few years before being phased out, beginning in 1978—except in the 82nd Airborne, where it continued to serve until quite recently.

DESCRIPTION

The Sheridan is only 20 feet 8 inches (6.3m) long, 9 feet 3 inches (2.8m) wide, and 9 feet 8 inches (2.9m) high. Its aluminum-alloy armor keeps its weight down to about 35,000 pounds (15,890kg), combat loaded. The tank exerts a ground pressure of about 7 psi.

Power is supplied by a Detroit turbo-charged water-cooled V-6 diesel

engine generating 300 hp at 2,800 rpm. That propells the M551 to 45 mph (72.4kph) on a good road and, since the Sheridan is amphibious, 3.6 mph (5.7kph) in the water. It can cross a ditch 8 feet 4 inches (2.5m) wide, climb an obstacle 33 inches (83.8cm) high, and negotiate a 60 percent grade.

The engine and transmission are at the rear of the hull, with the drive sprocket at the rear. The little tank uses torsion bar suspension, with five road wheels to a side, and no track return rollers. All that indicates agility, and the Sheridan has plenty of that. It was quick, small, and well suited to its recon assignment.

Layout for the crew is pretty conventional, although the big rounds take up a lot of space inside, cramping the crew.

One major worry for M551 crews is the caseless main gun ammunition. It is more prone to inadvertent detonation than the cased variety used on

OPPOSITE: Driver's compartment, M551. Visibility isn't much worse than any tank, buttoned up–three little vision blocks provide a peek outside. Steering is with a T-bar handle; the fore and aft is adjustable to suit your reach.
ABOVE: Quick, agile, with a very big gun, the little Sheridan was the paratrooper's best friend on the battlefield until very recently. This one is retired now and part of Jacques Littlefield's stable.

U.S. MBTs like the M60 and M1. The tank's armor is good only against .50cal heavy machine-gun fire. All the Sheridans deployed to the Gulf War managed to evade anti-armor threats, but the crews were sincerely worried.

WEAPONRY

The original idea behind the Sheridan was to combine a big weapon–to deal with any known potential armored threat–with a light chassis that could go anywhere. The selected weapon system, designated M81, was an innovative 152mm combination gun/guided missile. Unfortunately, the system was prematurely adopted before the bugs were worked out. In fact, many of those bugs were never quite exterminated.

The gun/launcher was a novel design for the U.S. Army, like much of the rest of the vehicle. The breech was power-actuated, unlike other recoil-operated cannons. The tube would elevate +19 degrees and depress to -8 degrees, with a full 360 -degree traverse in only ten seconds.

The MGM-51C Shillelagh missile, developed by Philco-Ford and the U.S. Army Missile Command during the 1960s and 1970s, flies downrange to the target, up to 3,800 yards (3,474.7m) away, using guidance commands transmitted by an IR system aboard the Sheridan. Once the gunner fires, the missile is ejected from the launcher by a gas generator. The solid-fuel rocket motor then ignites for a burn time of 1.18 seconds. Small fins pop out to help

LEFT: The armored basket for the commander was added after combat experience in Vietnam demonstrated its utility. The big IR searchlight is obsolete now that most armies have night-vision devices that make it show up like a beacon. **RIGHT:** Gunner's control panel, M551. The recoil from the huge gun was so powerful that the electronics for these systems were often knocked out. **BELOW:** Commander's over-ride and gun controls, M551.

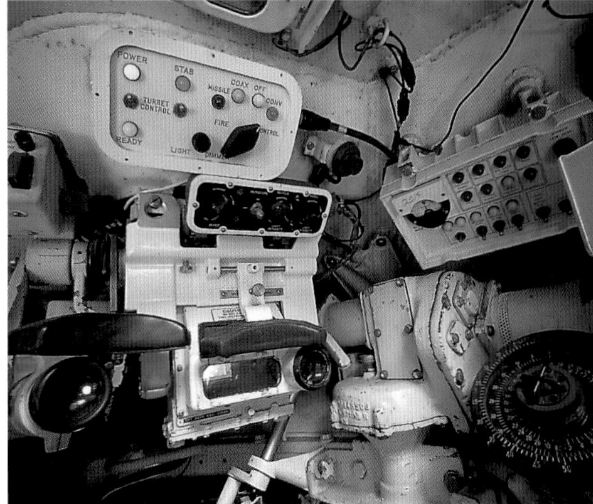

stabilize the missile in flight. The small guidance rocket kicks in for the rest of the flight, keeping the missile on target. The gunner keeps the sight aligned on the target center of mass while the 59-pound (26.7kg) weapon whooshes off on its mission, and IR signals keep it on course.

It was a good system, once the bugs were mostly worked out. It has been used only once in combat, effectively taking out an Iraqi bunker.

The same launcher can fire the 152mm caseless round. Although innovative and effective upon first combat usage, this round turned out to be another technological failure. The rounds are huge and difficult to manage in the turret, but that was the least of the problems crews had with the gun.

The system uses combustible cases. Upon firing, the projectile disappears downrange. All that was supposed to be left in the breech was a little stub from the cartridge case. To their horror, Sheridan crews discovered that the combustible cases didn't entirely combust. They opened the breech after a shot to find flaming debris falling into the turret. The risk of this debris setting fire to ready rounds in the turret was extreme.

That wasn't all. The caseless ammunition swelled in damp conditions, and a bump on a sharp object could break one open, spilling propellant all over the turret. The problem of burning debris was partially solved by

purging the tube with compressed air before cycling the breech, but the caseless ammunition continued to cause problems as long as the Sheridan was in service.

A full range of projectiles was developed for the 152mm gun: High Explosive Anti-Tank (HEAT), for dealing with enemy tanks, but also white phosphorus (WP) and canister rounds for use against troops in the open. Both of the latter rounds were quite useful in Vietnam. The vicious WP round sprays chunks of burning phosphorus—a very nasty material that is practically impossible to extinguish. It burns everything over a wide area. The canister round contains thousands of small steel arrows, each about the size of a nail. They will cut down an enemy infantry assault in platoon-size swaths.

There are virtues and drawbacks to combining a big gun with a light chassis. The recoil force from the Sheridan's gun is tremendous. The front of the tank comes 2 feet (61cm) off the ground, and the crew inside have reported recoil sensations approaching a religious experience. That recoil can jar electronic circuit boards loose in the fire control computer and rearrange anything on the vehicle not securely lashed down.

Besides the big guns, a very handy Ma Duce .50cal M2 heavy machine gun is installed above the TC's hatch. The TC can operate this gun remotely, from under armor, or standing exposed. As a result of combat experience in Vietnam in the early 1970s, an armored "bathtub" was added around the TC's cupola to protect against small-arms fire while operating the .50cal.

MISSIONS AND ASSIGNMENTS

The light weight of the M551 allowed the U.S. Army to do something unique

OPPOSITE: Turret detail, M551. Directly above the huge 152mm gun is the ballistic door, which protects the gunner's primary sight except when the crew are searching for and engaging targets. Four smoke grenade launchers are visible on the left. **RIGHT:** At just 35,000 pounds (15,890kg) and with a 300 hp engine, the Sheridan is a zippy little battlefield sports car, quite able to blow the doors off the competition.

with it: deliver armed combat power by parachute directly to an airhead behind enemy lines to support an airborne assault. It took special preparation and eight 100-foot (30.4m) cargo parachutes, but a C-130 could deliver both the Sheridan and its crew in one pass–the crew following the tank out the back of the C-130 and landing nearby. Once on the ground, the straps that attached the tank to its pallet and parachute were stripped. The men piled aboard, and then made the short commute to the combat zone.

Sheridans were originally supposed to be able to swim without preparation, but became prohibitively heavy during development. A permanently attached flotation screen erected around the hull prevented sinking.

The M551 Sheridan did a good job when it provided armored recon in Operation Just Cause, the 1989 invasion of Panama. It was among the first U.S. combat vehicles sent to Saudi Arabia at the outset of Operation Desert Shield during the summer of 1990, and fought with XVIII Airborne Corps in the Western Desert.

SPECIFICATIONS	M551 Sheridan
Crew	4
Weight	34,898 lbs (15.8t)
Length with gun forward	20 ft 8 in (6.3m)
Turret height	9 ft 8 in (2.9m)
Width	9 ft 3 in (2.8m)
Ground clearance	1 ft 7 in (48.3cm)
Ground pressure	6.96 lbs (3.16kg)
Propulsion	Detroit Diesel 6V53T 6-cylinder engine producing 300 hp at 2800 rpm
Transmission	Hydramatic torque converter with pivot steer capability
Speed	45 mph (72.4kph) (road), 3.6 mph (5.7kph) (water)
Acceleration	not available
Range	373 miles (600.1km)
Obstacle crossing	Vertical: 2 ft 9 in (83.8cm) Trench: 8 ft 4 in (2.5m)
Main armament	M81 152mm gun/launcher; MGM-51C missile
Co-axial weapon	7.62mm
Loader's weapon	none
Commander's weapon	.50cal machine gun M2, heavy barrel
NBC protection	Air filtration/mask system

THE SOVIET T-72

Prior to the beginning of ground combat in Operation Desert Storm, many observers fretted about what would happen when Iraq's Republican Guards and their T-72s actually fought American M1 Abrams and British Challenger II tanks. There was genuine concern that the T-72's great gun, excellent armor, and superb mobility could combine to create major problems for coalition forces. They need not have worried.

When actual combat between the T-72 and modern American and British tanks finally occurred, it was hardly a contest. The M1s blew the turrets right off the enemy tanks. Sabot rounds neatly penetrated the T-72's thick turret armor, and sometimes passed right through the tank.

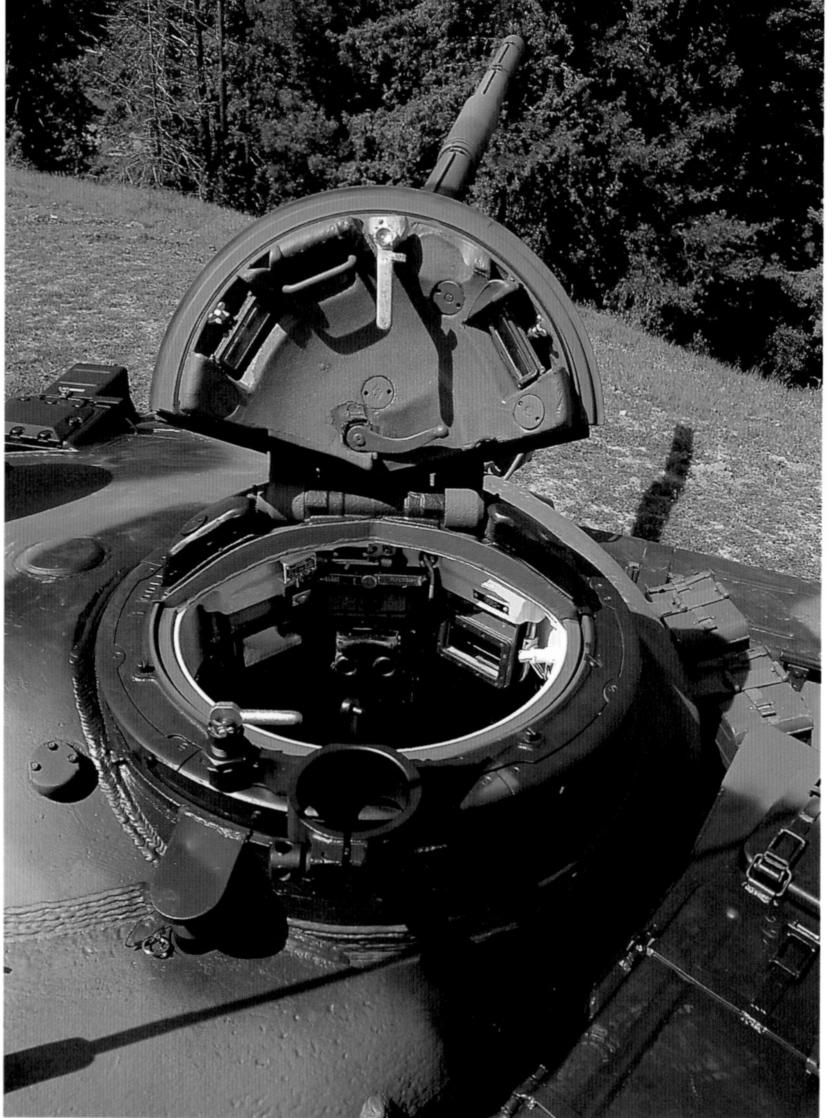

Few Iraqi tankers managed to fire on the Abrams before they were killed or had surrendered. No M1 Abrams were destroyed by those hits. It seemed almost unfair, particularly of course to the Iraqis.

Most Iraqi tank crews bailed out after a few seconds of battle with the Abrams. At one point, two T-72s were hit and started spouting fire out of the turret hatches, like twin 30-foot (9.1m) blowtorches. The surviving crews chose discretion over valor. Without the Abrams' thermal imaging systems, and without all the support available to Abrams tankers, the Iraqis were fighting blind–when they fought at all. A force of cold, hungry, demoralized, isolated tankers with obsolete weapons were fighting a well-armed and -supported force. That's no contest at all.

The T-72 is a much better tank than it appeared during the Gulf War, by which time it was aging. The T-72 is a Soviet version of the U.S. M60A1 tank, an earlier-generation combat

LEFT: Commander's hatch, T-72. The fit is remarkably tight with almost no room inside for the TC to move around. OPPOSITE: Only two T-72s are in private hands anywhere in the world, and this is one. It has been meticulously restored, inside and out. The gun doesn't fire–but the engine smokes just as badly as the ones in service with armies around the world.

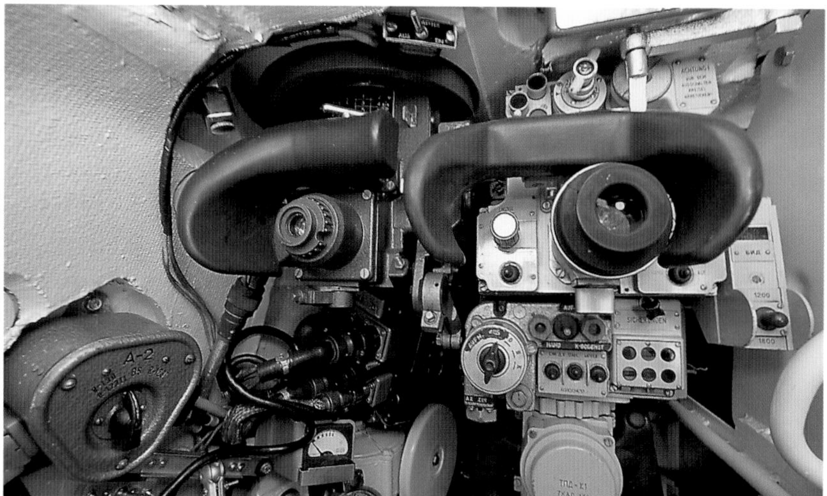

vehicle. It was an excellent tank when new. Today, a product improvement program has made it even better.

The T-72 is a typical Russian/ Soviet design: lots of armor and power, a big gun, a very low, sleek shape, and some very advanced features. It has a crew of three instead of four, thanks to a reasonably reliable automatic loader. It has a good laser range finder and good stabilization system, both on a par with the M60A1 it was intended to fight.

DESIGN HISTORY

The T-72 is a direct descendant of the T-62 and used many components and design standards of its ancestor. Development was done at the Morozov Design Bureau, headed by Valeriy Venediktov. Production began in 1971, and the new design was first revealed in 1977 when the French Minister of Defense visited the Tamanskaya Guards Division, a unit equipped with the tank. Western observers got a better look at the T-72 a month later when the tank appeared in a parade in Red Square.

The result within NATO was something like panic. The T-72 was obviously a new system, with a huge gun, but its subsystems were a mystery.

The T-72 was used in combat by Syria against the Israelis in 1982, and then by Iraq in 1991, yet neither time with much success.

About twenty thousand T-72s have been built, in many variants, for home and export. Additional armor was applied to the turret front of the T-72 B (the "Dolly Parton" model), and even more to the T-72 B1 (the "Super Dolly Parton"). Reactive armor–small blocks of explosive that detonate when struck by HEAT rounds, RPG warheads, and similar "chemical energy" warheads–was installed on many recent variants.

BASICS

Only three crewmen operate the T-72: driver, gunner, and TC. The loader's job is performed by an automatic mechanical system. While there are advantages to reducing crew size in combat, there are handicaps as well. One less man is available to help rearm and refuel, to stand guard at night, and to take care of maintenance chores. Inevitably, those chores are often done by only two men since the TC will be called away to perform other leadership duties. The remaining crew is bound to be more tired and stressed, neither of which helps crew performance or combat efficiency.

HOW TO DRIVE THE T-72

Well, enough of specifications and data–let's fire up a T-72 and take it for a spin. First, climb aboard. The front glacis plate is low, and that makes the tank easy to mount. You can clamber up from the side or just jump up on the glacis plate if you're a young tanker in good shape.

The driver's hatch cover pops up and pivots to the right for entry. Climb in and settle down into the seat. It will probably be set for driving with the hatch open and head exposed. A latch on the left side releases the catch for the seat, which is spring-loaded, and you can adjust it to suit yourself, then secure the latch to lock the position. Tank drivers need to be able to button up almost instantly, so seat adjustment is a regular part of the drill.

OPPOSITE: Gunner's sight systems, T-72. Some of the controls are accessible only by touch–they are completely out of sight unless you contort yourself in the tight spaces. ABOVE: Jacques Littlefield's T-72, fresh from its complete overhaul.

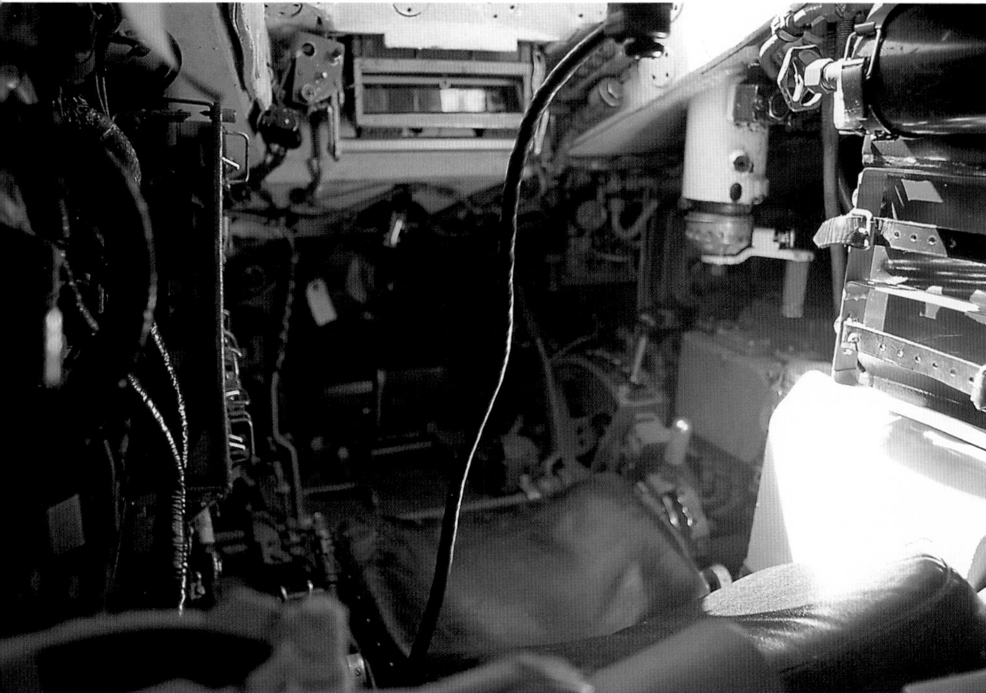

LEFT: Driver's compartment, T-72. The driver has the most comfortable station on the tank but he needs to be a brute to drive the vehicle at low speeds. BELOW: An "anti-spall" liner on the inside of the hatch and the rest of the turret helps protect the crew from some penetrations, but only against small shards. American and British sabot "long rod" penetrators easily defeated the T-72's armor during Desert Storm.

The driver's compartment and controls are quite conventional. You sit in the center of the hull. When driving with the hatch closed, or "buttoned up," you use a wide-field TVNE-4E periscope. On early models, an IR viewer is available for use at night in conjunction with the IR searchlight, and passive night-vision systems are provided on more recent versions. The periscope pops out and locks in place with two latches, one on each side of the aperture.

An instrument panel is on your left. On export models, like Jacques Littlefield's former East German G model (the German army still has some, but they sold or scrapped others), most instruments will be lettered in the language of the purchasing country, but you can figure them out pretty quickly–ammeter, oil pressure, tach, speedometer, and odometer.

The big gearshift lever is on your right, along with the hand throttle. The gear lever is marked 0 (neutral) through 6 forward, and reverse.

To fire up the tank's big V-12 engine, first make sure the transmission is in neutral, set the brake, then open the air line valve. It is blue, on your right and up by the controls for the driver's hatch. Turn the electrical master switch to ON. Then you need to pump up the diesel-fuel purging system. There's a lever for that on the right side. Pump fifteen or twenty times until you can feel it pressurize and the lever gets hard to operate. Move the hand throttle, on your right side down on the deck behind the gear lever, from the IDLE CUT OFF position to the START detent, a notch or two forward.

The START switch is on the instrument panel on your left side, toward the front. It is a two-piece switch, both covered with spring-loaded guards that you must raise before the buttons can be depressed. Press the two buttons together. All that happens at first is the distant whine of a motor somewhere back in the engine compartment. That's the engine pre-oiler lubing the cylinder walls. It has a built-in timer that operates for a few seconds. After the engine has been prelubed, the

electric starter automatically kicks in. The engine will ordinarily fire right up.

In cold weather, however, battery performance can be insufficient to start the engine. All Russian tanks have optional pneumatic starting, a cold-proof system. To air-start the tank, push the AIR START button, a blue control above your right shoulder. Compressed air will be fed into the engine, spinning it easily. Without any input from you, the engine controls will preheat the fuel and cylinders and the engine will rumble to life with a throaty growl and a cloud of blue oil smoke.

Allow the engine to warm to operating temperature, and leave the air line valve open. A small compressor will recharge the cylinder. You don't need to close the valve until you shut the engine down.

While waiting for the engine to warm, monitor the instruments for oil pressure and current flow. Keep the rpm down. After a few minutes, with the coolant and oil temperatures up in the normal range, you're ready to go. Move the hand throttle back to reduce idle rpm to a normal range. Release the parking brake, grab the steering levers, and put your foot on the brake. When you're ready to move out, depress the clutch and shift into first. Let out the clutch, release the foot brake, and step on the accelerator.

Off you go!

The steering controls have hydraulic power boost. They're lighter than manual controls found on earlier

JACQUES LITTLEFIELD ON THE T-72

Jacques Littlefield owns one of only two T-72 tanks in private hands (shown in the accompanying photographs) and has what must be one of the best collection of military and armored vehicles anywhere. Here's what he has to say about the T-72:

The T-72 drives better than other Russian tanks—the transmission is easier to operate. I like driving it, once you get used to the lag in control input, but it isn't as nice to drive as an M1 or M60. Steering doesn't require much effort, and control is good at all speeds.

Mobility on the T-72 is good. The laser range finder and gun systems all seem to be okay for 1970s technology, although the night-vision systems aren't as good as in the M1.

The real problem with the tank is ammunition stowage. It is deadly. That's because it isn't protected the way it is in the M1. The separate loading ammunition is very vulnerable to a turret penetration.

Also, because of the way the turret is configured, the TC's visibility to the rear seems much more restricted than in the M60 or M1. He can see to the rear if he's standing out of the hatch, but if he's seated there doesn't seem to be a way to rotate the cupola to see to the rear. That's not the case in the other tanks. That's because the T-72 commander can't stand inside the turret. There just isn't room. So visibility is a problem.

Another problem is that the armor isn't very thick on some versions—although the Russians have added some to later versions—and it's homogenous rather than composite Chobham-type.

Then there's the ammunition. Norinco, the Chinese ammunition manufacturing company, makes and sells rounds for both the 120mm Rheinmetall gun round, and the 125mm round used on the T-72. According to their literature, the 120mm round achieves better penetration—550mm (22 inches) of homogenous steel armor at 0 degrees at 2,000 meters (2,187 yards)—than the 125mm round which will penetrate about 450mm (18 inches) under the same conditions.

Last but not least, the auto-loader has a cycle time of about 12.5 seconds. A trained M1 loader can cut that time in half or more!

So, generally, it is an older-generation tank. Its rate of fire is slow. It has less armor protection than NATO tanks. It is vulnerable to sneak attacks from the rear because of poor visibility provisions for the commander.

But if you put a single T-72 up against a single M60, or an M60A1, bet on the T-72. Between a T-72 and a M60A3, take the A3 because it has better accuracy. If the 72 got a hit on a M60 of any variant, it would knock it out—but the reverse is true, too. Up against any of the really modern Western tanks, like the Challenger 2 or the "Leo," the T-72 wouldn't stand a chance.

10011

LEFT: Alan Cors is the other private owner of a T-72–and his has a mine plow. This tank and many others in the Cors collection are used in motion pictures, TV commercials, and occasional public displays.

tanks, but there is a momentary lag between input and response that can be a little disconcerting. You quickly get used to it, though, and anticipate the delay. The T-72 is agile and responsive, in spite of all that weight and bulk, and accelerates, turns, and brakes quickly. You have to work up through each of the gears in turn, without skipping any–although you'll rarely get above fourth or fifth.

The gunner's position is to the left of the gun, and very close to the breech and automatic loader. There were reports of injuries to gunners and TCs of T-72 tanks whose arms got caught in the loading mechanism. Even Charles Lemon, director of the Patton Tank Museum at Fort Knox, Kentucky, had a close call with one.

The gunner's position gives him very little room to move around. It is no surprise that T-72 crewmen often stood in their turret hatches rather than sitting inside. His hatch folds forward, providing some protection against snipers and small-arms fire from the front.

Many of the gunner's controls are out of sight and he has to feel around for them, but their location become second nature to him anyway. The advantage of close quarters is that all the gunner's controls are within easy reach. The Abrams gunner, by contrast, had to turn to his right, away from his sight and controls, to make entries in the ballistics computer. The T-72 gunner doesn't have to move to make the same entries.

The basic T-72's gunner has a TNP-160 periscope and TNPA65 vision block for search and target acquisition. He also has a TDP-2-49 daylight sight plus a TPN 1-49-23 night system. The sight system's range finder, a stereoscopic type on early models, is supposed to be accurate to 3,800 yards (3,474.7m), and the sight itself has vertical axis stabilization. Laser range finders are installed on more recent models, including the early G model T-72 pictured.

While some sources claim maximum effective ranges for the gun/sight/range-finder system of 3,800 yards (3,474.7m) for sabot antitank rounds and 4,800 yards (4,389.1m) for HE fragmentation rounds, the U.S. Army's published specs for the T-72 give it credit for just 1,900 yards (1,737.3m) maximum effective range for direct-fire missions. The gun can also be used for indirect fire out to about 9,000 yards (8,229.6m) when the standard-issue quadrant is installed on the breech and conventional artillery fire mission procedures are used.

The T-72 has an infrared searchlight for night vision. This was a good feature twenty years ago, but a sure way to become a target today. That searchlight now shows up vividly on thermal night-vision devices. IR driving lights were installed on the glacis plate, adding several hundred feet (about 100m) of night visibility ahead.

C H A P T E R E L E V E N

THE MERKEVA: CHARIOT OF FIRE

The technological focus of armored vehicle development since World War II has been on NATO and the WarPac nations. Yet the real battlefield lessons have come from Israel via her many confrontations with Egypt, Jordan, Syria, and the PLO in Lebanon. American, British, and French tanks have been designed, produced in quantity, issued to the troops for years, then declared obsolete—all without seeing actual combat. Israeli tanks and tankers were not able to get away with that. They learned their lessons the hard way—at war.

Today, the Merkeva is one of the world's most radical MBTs. Its shape and substance are the direct result of battlefield experience. Much of that seminal experience occurred during the 1967 war against the United Arab Republic. Israel's obsolete British Centurions, American M48s, and even WWII Shermans faced squadrons of new Russian T-55s. Israel won those tank battles, but at a high cost in men and machines.

After the war, an arms embargo prevented Israel from buying modern tanks from France and England. It was several years before the U.S. allowed M60s to be exported. That left Israel to its own resources; thus a state-of-the-art Israeli MBT was developed. The project began in 1967. In 1970 General Israel Tal—Six-Day War hero and armored force commander—took charge of development. Prototypes appeared in 1977, production tanks in 1979. The new MBT went into battle against the PLO in Lebanon during the summer of 1982.

Just about everything on the Merkeva is unusual. The engine, for example, is not in the rear. It is set in front and on the right side, its mass providing additional "armor" protection for the crew in the fighting compartment.

Its design stresses armored protection rather than speed and agility, a

lesson from earlier wars. The vehicle is extremely low, only about 8½ feet (2.5m) to the top of the turret roof. The tank is so low that the tube is only 6 feet (1.8m) off the ground during normal-range engagements. A Merkeva can hide behind almost any size berm or depression in the terrain with almost no exposure to counter-fire. The turret shape is small and slender. Both features help to make the Merkeva a small target for enemy tanks or TOW missile teams.

Unlike virtually every other MBT, the Merkeva can accommodate a few infantry and "de-bus" them to engage enemy dismounts through a hatch at the rear of the tank. That same hatch allows the Merkeva crew to recover battlefield casualties with much more protection than armored ambulances like the Warrior or Bradley variants.

OPPOSITE: This is a dangerous view of the Merkeva, the last thing a lot of Arab gunners saw just before everything went black.
ABOVE: The Merkeva is designed to do two things exceptionally well: keep the crew safe, and be very dangerous to any enemy within about 2 miles (3.2km).

Another important Merkeva innovation is a 60mm Soltam mortar, an indirect-fire weapon that uses HE, illumination, and smoke rounds. The mortar, fired from within the turret, could engage unseen targets with its lobbing rounds. Thirty rounds for this weapon are carried.

Israeli tanks were frequently hit and disabled by RPG and Sagger missile hits coming in under the turret bustle, detonating against the turret ring, and knocking out the tank. As an antidote to this tactic, Merkeva comes equipped with a row of chains with steel balls on the end, all around the turret bustle. Any shaped-charge weapon striking these will detonate well before their warheads are close enough to be fully effective.

The Merkeva's Teledyne Continental V-12 diesel engine produces 900 hp for the Mk 1, and up to 1200 hp for the latest Mk 4 version.

RIGHT: **Israeli tankers have far more successful combat experience than any other modern military force, in places like the Golan Heights (as shown here) and elsewhere, and that experience has shaped this extremely capable tank.**

SPECIFICATIONS	Merkeva (Chariot) Mk 3
Crew	4
Weight	132,000 lbs (59.8t) (combat loaded)
Length with gun forward	28 ft (8.5m)
Turret height	8 ft 6 in (2.5m)
Width	12 ft (3.6m)
Ground clearance	1 ft 7 in (48.2cm)
Ground pressure	.96 kg/cm^2
Propulsion	1200-hp Teledyne Continental AVDS-1790-9AR air-cooled diesel
Transmission	Ashot fully automatic, electronic control
Speed	34 mph (54.7kph)
Range	310 miles (498.7km)
Obstacle crossing	Vertical: 3 ft (91.4cm) Trench: 11 ft 6 in (3.5m)
Main armament	120mm smoothbore; 50 rounds carried
Co-axial weapon	7.62mm
Loader's weapon	7.62mm
Commander's weapon	7.62mm
NBC protection–all threats	Overpressure with central filter and air conditioning

SAM KATZ ON THE MERKEVA

SAM KATZ is an author and authority on Israeli military systems and operations. Here are his comments on the Merkeva.

The Merkeva was the product of General Israel Tal—and of the deaths of numerous Israeli tank crews killed in old WWII and subpar Western tanks during the 1967 war. Egyptian armor wasn't very effective in that war but a lot of Israeli tanks were hit and destroyed by dug-in anti-tank guns. Many of the six hundred–plus Israeli soldiers killed in that war were tankers. Those deaths started the Merkeva's design process.

General Tal was one of the heroes of the '67 war, and it was his idea to produce a homegrown tank that would exactly fit Israeli requirements. He wanted to prevent Israel from being dependent on England and the U.S. for modern equipment. That was the basic idea behind Merkeva, which in Hebrew means "Chariot."

The hatch at the rear of the tank was another result of combat experience, this time from the 1973 war. Israel had many tanks ambushed in the Sinai desert and the Golan Heights by mobile commando teams. Syria and Egypt flew these teams in between the lines at night, by helicopter—ten or fifteen guys with RPGs and Sagger missiles. Then they would wreak havoc the next day, knocking out a lot of tanks and creating many casualties. So the Merkeva was designed to carry small infantry teams into places where these commandos were likely to be and to conduct counter-ambush operations. It was also useful for evacuating casualties from the battlefield, under fire—and it was the safest way for the tank crew to get out under fire when the Merkeva was disabled in combat.

Against the PLO and Syrians in Lebanon, the old Mk 1s did extremely well against the T-55s and T-62s. Some of the Merkevas took hits, but—unlike in previous wars, when Israel used "war surplus" tanks—very few tank crewmen were killed by enemy action. Merkeva also has the distinction of being the first Western tank to destroy a T-72.

The new Mk 3 is rumored to be equal to or superior to the M1A2 Abrams. It is supposed to be the only tank in the world capable of tracking and engaging moving targets while it is moving at full speed. It has a thermal and daylight video sighting system able to "lock on" moving targets, similar to the TADS systems used on modern attack aircraft. This system has been used to lock on and destroy a Syrian helicopter in flight.

Some Merkevas in Lebanon were beat up badly by Syrian Gazelle attack helicopters firing AT missiles and cannon. While the tank's main gun was normally the best weapon to use against these targets, there were times when the crew was busy engaging an armor threat of higher priority. In those cases, the .50cal machine gun was the weapon of choice. The best place for this weapon, it turned out, wasn't the normal pintle mount by the TC's hatch, but up on the front of the turret, mounted low. The machine gunner stretched out atop the turret and fired from the prone position.

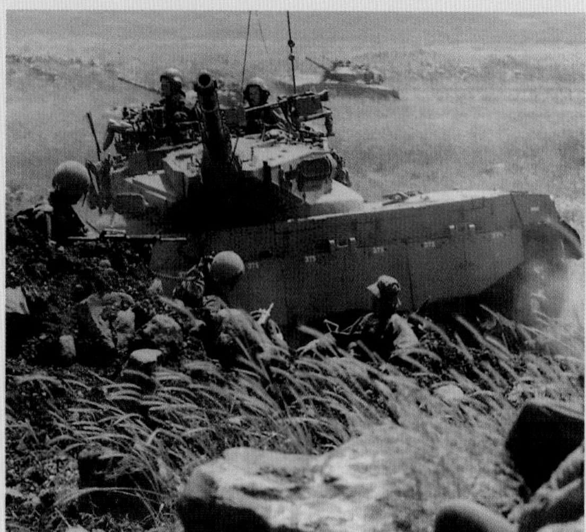

LEFT: Israel learned the hard way how important infantry-armor cooperation is on the modern battlefield, as this squad of infantry and a tank platoon demonstrate in the Golan. OPPOSITE: Merkeva can provide battlefield taxi service for three infantrymen or recon scouts—handy passengers when enemy anti-tank teams need to be dug out of bunkers and trenches.

1

CHAPTER TWELVE

THE CHALLENGER 2

The superb Challenger 2 is currently Britain's MBT, a state-of-the-art 60-ton (54.4t) combat vehicle built by Vickers Defence Systems. The Challenger 2 program began in 1986 and design work finished in 1989. The British government ordered 127 tanks, enough for only two regiments. Since then, the tank has been promoted for export sales; the nation of Oman has purchased twenty-two of them. Although not nearly as common as the U.S. Abrams tanks, which have been built by the thousands, the Challenger 2 is among the world's most advanced and capable MBTs.

The turret and hull are set up conventionally for a crew of four: driver, loader, gunner, and commander–with the driver forward in the hull and the other three in the fighting compartment. Another advanced feature is the 120mm L30 gun, part of the CHARM (challenger armament) system. The barrel is manufactured by Royal Ordnance Nottingham. It was the first British tube to be chrome-lined, a process that reduced wear and prolonged barrel life.

Like the Russian T-72, the Challenger 2 uses two-part ammunition, with propellant and projectile loaded separately. Ammunition is

RIGHT: Britain's superb Challenger at speed. Challenger is claimed by some authorities to be technically superior to the M1A2 Abrams. British armor and cannon technology certainly has led the rest of the world during recent years.
BELOW: Severely sloped frontal armor helps deflect enemy rounds, but the advanced "Chobham" composite material does even more. This is a very difficult tank to kill with any kind of modern ground anti-tank weapon.

35KA76
78

LEFT: While the gun and armor are state-of-the-art, Challenger still uses a conventional–but very powerful–diesel engine for propulsion, unlike the Abrams and its gas turbine. It is otherwise a very modern, capable, and expensive combat vehicle.

stowed low in the hull, well below the turret and in armored stowage containers, to help protect against catastrophic explosions when the tank is penetrated by enemy fire. Fifty-two rounds of main gun ammo are carried, plus four thousand 7.62mm rounds for the co-axial and loader's machine guns. The co-ax, unlike most other modern tanks, is a high-rate-of-fire chain gun from Hughes Helicopter.

Challenger 2 is powered by a huge Perkins 1200-hp diesel engine, driving a T54 transmission, with six forward and two reverse gear ratios. This drivetrain propels the tank to 35 mph (56.3kph) road and 24 (38.6kph) mph off road. The track tension can be adjusted by the driver from inside his compartment using a hydraulic control–something done previously while lying in the mud, wrestling with massive wrenches.

SPECIFICATIONS	Challenger 2
Crew	4
Weight	137,500 lbs (62.5t)
Length with gun forward	38 ft (11.5m)
Turret height	8 ft 3 in (2.5m)
Width	11 ft 6 in (3.5m)
Ground clearance	1 ft 7 in (48.2cm)
Ground pressure	5.0 lbs (2.29kg)
Propulsion	Perkins Condor V-12, 1200-hp air-cooled diesel
Transmission	David Brown T54; six forward, two reverse gears
Speed	35 mph (56.3kph), 24 mph (38.6kph) cross-country
Range	250 miles (402.2km)
Obstacle crossing	Vertical: 2 ft 10 in (86.3cm) Trench: 7 ft 6 in (2.2m)
Main armament	120mm L30
Co-axial weapon	7.62mm
Loader's weapon	7.62mm
Commander's weapon	7.62mm
NBC protection–all threats	Overpressure

CHAPTER THIRTEEN

THE M1 ABRAMS

The M1 Abrams is one of those "they said it couldn't be done" military success stories, a tank that the skeptics were convinced, back in the 1970s, would never be able to fulfill its sponsor's promises.

The Abrams uses a 1500-hp gas turbine engine, the kind found on helicopters and aircraft, instead of a proper diesel engine like virtually all other tanks. It uses a highly complex, computer-based, integrated fire-control system that measures everything from wind speed to the microscopic warp of the barrel under the noonday sun. The M1 Abrams, unlike almost all other tanks today, abandoned cast-steel hull and turret designs for a fabricated structure built from slabs of exotic layered armor. It is big, expensive, complicated, and the best tank in the world, even today. When it dominated the competition during Desert Storm, the critics finally shut up.

Development of the Abrams began in 1971 with the XM1 and the U.S. Army's request for an MBT to replace the aging but otherwise excellent M60 series. The basic mission of the XM1 was to confront the Red Horde in northern Europe and to defeat a threatened armored attack by forces of the Warsaw Pact, the kickoff for the long-anticipated third world war. The production contract for the tank, officially named M1 Abrams, was awarded to Chrysler Defense Incorporated, later taken over by General Dynamics.

Fundamental requirements for the M1 were that it had to: 1) dominate the battlefield with its gun, 2) be highly mobile and agile, 3) have a very high degree of protection for its crew; and 4) be economically feasible. The unit cost began at $500,000 per vehicle–a bargain at the time.

RIGHT: On the road again, an M1 from the 4th Infantry Division dashes forward during training at Fort Carson, Colorado. LEFT: A peek through the Gunner's Primary Sight (GPS) reveals a target well within range. The reticule is aligned with the target's "center of mass" and a hit is virtually guaranteed.

DESCRIPTION

In keeping with contemporary thoughts about tank design, the Abrams is big, fast, and low. It is more than 32 feet (9.7m) long (with the gun tube forward) and 12 feet (3.6m) wide. When filled with fuel, ammo, and

crew, it tips the scales at 63 tons (57.1t). Despite the massive size and weight, the Abrams has excellent agility and a very good power-to-weight ratio: 27 hp to the ton (908kg).

There is a four-man crew: driver, loader, gunner, and commander. The driver sits in the center of the vehicle, in a reclining position. His steering control is a T-bar similar to that on a motorcycle. The rotary throttle control is the same as on a Harley-Davidson.

The instrumentation is typical, with a few exceptions. Instead of magnetos, the Abrams gas turbine engine fires up with a push button. The start sequence is entirely automatic—as was much of the operation of the tank.

The M1A1 and A2 versions use a very large 120mm smoothbore gun that fires a projectile downrange at about a mile (1.6km) per second. Anyone in the vicinity of one when it fires regrets it. The effect of the gun is tremendous. There is a roar that sounds like the end of the world, accompanied by a fireball 20 feet (6m) across. The tracer element, a small bit of phosphorus in a cavity at the back of the projectile, marks the

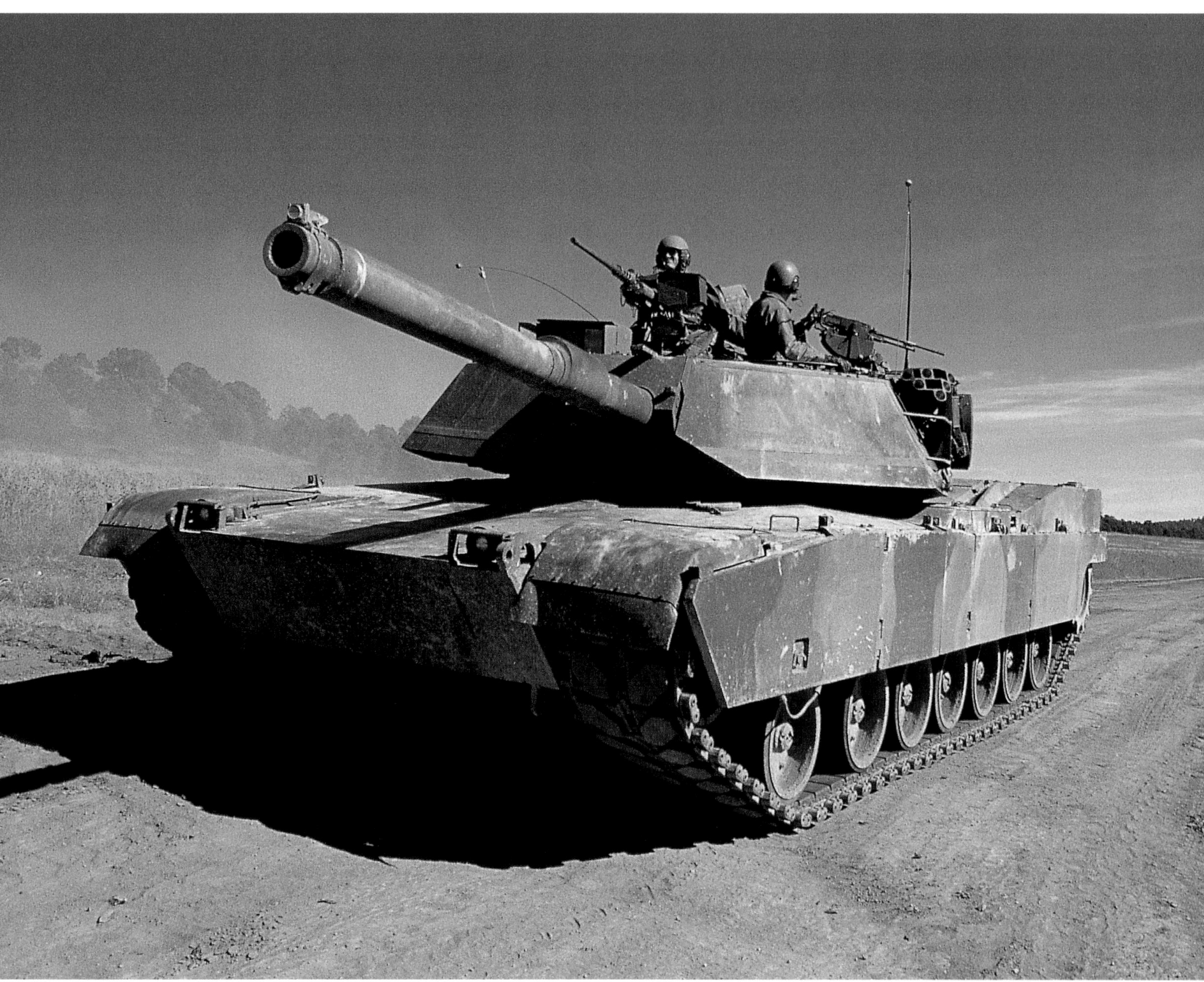

path of the round as it streaks toward the target—a fast, pure, straight line with a fireball on one end and a dust cloud and secondary explosion on the other. It is awesome.

The Lycoming Textron AGT 1500-hp engine that initially caused the skeptics so much concern ended up working extremely well. It is reliable, compact, easy to maintain, runs on almost anything, and will push the 63-ton (57.1) vehicle along at 42 mph (67.5kph). The engine is very quiet, particularly when compared to Soviet designs. The loudest sounds you hear from the Abrams as it dashes past is the squeak of the tracks and a subtle whine from the jet engine.

On the rare occasions when it needs serious attention, the engine slides out of its compartment on rails. The electrical connections, control linkages, and fuel lines all come apart at quick-disconnects. Swapping an engine takes about an hour and a half.

Much of the success of the Abrams in the Gulf War had to do with its very advanced thermal sight and laser range-finder system, which allows the gunner or TC to see, identify, and engage targets through dust storms, smoke clouds, and gloom of night—all with great precision.

The Abrams was designed to provide excellent crew protection. The "Chobham" layered armor, developed by the British, effectively insulates the M1 crewmen from enemy fire.

OPPOSITE: All Abrams tanks use the same basic "Chobham" composite armor as invented by the British. In the most current A2 version this composite armor is reported to include depleted uranium. **RIGHT:** On the way! A M1A1 launches a round downrange at a velocity of more than 1 mile (1.6km) per second, propelled on its way by a 20-foot (6m) fireball. **BELOW:** No rest for the weary: a crew replenishes main gun and machine-gun ammunition. This is a HEAT round.

There is more to the design, however, than just hull and turret armor. All the main gun ammunition is stowed behind sliding ballistic doors at the rear of the turret, isolated from the fighting compartment. In the event of an enemy hit that penetrated the armor and detonated the ammunition, two ballistic panels on the top of the turret would blow off, venting the force of the explosion away from the crew.

MODIFICATIONS

Modifications have improved the Abrams over the years. The first major improvement came in 1985 with the M1A1. This model has improved armor, a larger 120mm gun, modifications to the drivetrain, an integrated NBC (protection against nuclear, biological, and chemical warfare) system, and other changes. Depleted uranium, a material more than twice as dense as steel, was added to the armor of the 1988 version of the M1A1. The uranium was part of a projectile-resistant, multilayer sandwich of armor.

A major improvement program for the Abrams began in 1988. This resulted in the M1A2 version. The A2 has much-improved imaging systems for the commander and gunner, a data link to allow the tank to send information to aircraft, GPS navigation, a better weapons system for the commander, and improved suspension.

COMBAT EXPERIENCE

While seven M1 tanks took hits from enemy tanks during Operation Desert Storm, none was penetrated by those hits. That was partly because the Iraqis were using the least capable anti-armor rounds available for their 125mm guns. The Iraqis used sabot rounds with steel penetrators, rather

RIGHT: A platoon of Abrams waits to move up to the firing line at Fort Carson.

than the tungsten or depleted uranium rods used in higher grade ammunition. While these Iraqi sabot rounds were adequate for older targets–like the T-55s and Chieftains fielded by Iran in their earlier war–they didn't work against Chobham-type armor on the rare occasions when the Iraqis were able to hit a target.

Eight other tanks were damaged during combat operations, mostly by anti-tank mines. Four of these were disabled, and four damaged and repaired.

During the one-hundred–hour combat phase of Operation Desert Storm, the M1 Abrams tank units reported readiness rates exceeding 90 percent.

Abrams tanks are now in use in Egypt, where they are assembled from kits supplied by General Dynamics, and in Kuwait.

SPECIFICATIONS	M1 ABRAMS
Crew	4
Weight	126,000lbs (57.1t)
Length with gun forward	32 ft 3 in (9.8m)
Turret height	93½ inches (2.3m)
Width	12 ft 6 in (3.6m)
Ground clearance	1 ft 7 in (48.2cm)
Ground pressure	13.8 lbs (6.27kg)
Propulsion	Gas turbine engine, 1500 hp
Transmission	Hydrokinetic transmission; four forward, two reverse gears
Maximum governed speed	42 mph (67.5kph))
Speed cross-country	30 mph (48.2kph)
Speed 10% slope	20 mph (32.1kph)
Speed 60% slope	4.5 mph (7.2kph)
Range	275 miles (442.4km) cruising
Obstacle crossing	Vertical: 3 ft 6 in (1.1m) Trench: 9 feet (2.7m)
Main armament	120mm smoothbore cannon, XM256
Co-axial weapon	7.62mm machine gun, M240
Loader's weapon	7.62mm machine gun, M240, on Skate mount
Commander's weapon	.50cal machine gun, M2, on powered rotary platform
NBC protection	200 cu ft/minute, clean cooled air

31

HOW TO DRIVE THE M1 ABRAMS

Okay, enough with the history lesson and the facts and figures. Let's hop in an M1 Abrams, fire it up, and drive it around our own private training area.

First, you enter through the loader's hatch, up on the turret. Step on the loader's seat post, then drop down to the turret floor. Swing the loader's toe guard back–it forms a kind of gate–and slide feet-first into the driver's seat. You'll be in a reclining position; it's pretty dark with the hatch closed.

First, check all the switches on the Auxiliary Systems panel on your right. Personnel heater, night periscope, gas particle filter, bilge pump, smoke generator, lights, high beam, and tactical idle switches should all be in the OFF position. Check the fire extinguisher panel on the left. The red cover should be closed, the gauges at zero, and the tank selector to REAR.

Pull out and set the VEHICLE MASTER POWER switch to ON, then release. This energizes the electrical system by connecting the battery. The MASTER POWER light will illuminate. Then check the breaker box on your right. All breakers should read ON. The MASTER WARNING light above the T-bar steering control will be on, but that's normal. Press the RESET button on its panel and it will go out again. The electrical system gauge on the left, below the fire control panel, should indicate in the green.

Check for fuel in the tanks. The gauge and tank selector switch is on the left panel, and should be full. Anything less than a quarter full will get you a LOW FUEL LEVEL light. Then check the hydraulic pressure gauge for bleed-off. Some drop while parked is normal, but it should be within 1,000 to 1,700 psi.

Now it's time to put on your Combat Vehicle Crewman (known to the crews as a "CVC") helmet, plug in the lead to the internal communication system (ICS) control box, and set the switch to INT ONLY (to keep your squeals from being transmitted over the radio). The mike element should be adjusted to about 1 inch (2.5cm) in front of your mouth. The switch on the left side of the helmet should be set to the rear position.

Adjust the seat and headrest to suit yourself. Do the same with the three periscopes. Adjust periscopes so that you see the front slope of the tank at the very bottom of the field of view. Open the hatch with the lever on your right. Make sure it locks. Adjust your seat so that you're sitting upright, head out of the hatch.

To start the engine, call the TC on the ICS and tell him you're ready to fire up. He must ensure nobody's behind the tank during starting because of exhaust gas danger. Center the T-bar. Otherwise, the tank will pivot when the engine starts. The ENGINE START button is on the right control panel. Press and hold it for about three seconds, then release. You'll hear the turbine spin up, then a soft whoosh as it lights off. That's really all there is to it.

After a minute or so the engine will be warmed up. The tach will read about 925 rpm. The ELECTRICAL SYSTEM gauge should show about 28 volts. The MASTER WARNING and brake lights should be illuminated. Check the brakes by pressing hard on the pedal, which is in the normal spot. The brake pedal should feel solid. Set the transmission control (in the center of the T-bar) to D for drive, just like in your car.

Okay, here we go. Once you're in gear, release the foot brake and apply power, and you're on your way. Although the beast weighs about thirty times more than a common automobile, it is about as quick and responsive. You steer with the T-bar. After checking out the steering and trying the brakes, give it a little gas and roam around the training area. It is quite comfortable across open ground at up to 20 mph (32.1kph), depending on the terrain. Those long tracks even out the bumps very well. Now find a suitable level spot and bring the tank to a smooth halt.

Here's your next thrill: a pivot turn. With the throttle back to idle, the turbine will slowly return to idle speed, a delay of about thirty seconds. Shift the transmission control on the T-bar from D to PVT (pivot). The pivot turn is accomplished when the tracks move in opposite directions. Now apply power gradually and move the T-bar to the left or right. The tank rotates on its vertical axis, a 63-ton (57.1t) monster doing a graceful pirouette.

Okay, back to idle, center the T-bar, then shift back to D. Driver, move out! As you rumble across the terrain you will inevitably encounter small ditches, berms, logs, low walls, culverts, and anti-tank obstacles. It is quite possible to throw a track on any of these if you attempt to cross them improperly. The proper way is, normally, head-on, at a right angle to the obstacle, in low gear, and at a slow speed.

The same basic advice applies to hills. The Abrams will go up or down a 60 percent (31-degree) grade without trouble–if you go straight up or down, not at an angle across the slope. If you must traverse a slope, 40 percent (22-degree angle) is the maximum safe value to avoid sliding and possibly rolling the vehicle.

The tank will cross a fairly sizable obstacle–a flattened truck, perhaps, or a pile of rubble up to 3½ feet (1.1m) high. To cross such a vertical obstacle, slow down, warn the crew so that they can hold on, and ask the gunner to elevate the gun tube all the way. Put the transmission in low range, then drive forward slowly at a right angle to the obstacle. Once you start up and over, increase power, then slack off as the tank reaches its balance point on the obstacle. Ease the tank forward off the obstacle, using the brake as required for control. Once the tracks are back on the ground, shift back into D and continue the advance.

Good job, soldier. You've passed your M1 Abrams driving test.

BELOW: This lieutenant from the Georgia National Guard and his unit have come to the National Training Center at Fort Irwin, California, to learn large-unit battle tactics during nonstop three-week rotations.

PART TWO

OTHER MILITARY VEHICLES

WHILE THE MAIN BATTLE TANKS GET MOST OF THE ATTENTION, BOTH ON AND OFF THE BATTLEFIELD, EVERY MODERN ARMY FIELDS NUMEROUS SUPPORTING VEHICLES. SOME OF THESE ARE DESIGNED FOR COMBAT, LIKE FAST SCOUT VEHICLES WITH BIG GUNS AND THIN ARMOR, WHILE OTHERS ARE THIN-SKINNED SUPPORT VEHICLES LIKE TRUCKS AND FUEL TANKERS. THERE ARE JEEPS, "HUMMERS," DESERT PATROL VEHICLES, CONVERTED CIVILIAN UTILITY VEHICLES, MASSIVE RADAR VANS, RADIO TRUCKS, AMMUNITION CARRIERS, ANTI-AIRCRAFT GUN CARRIERS, HALF-TRACKS, AND MANY OTHERS, ALL BACKING UP THE ARMOR AND INFANTRY AND ARTILLERY, ONE WAY OR ANOTHER.

THE DEVELOPMENT OF THESE "COMBAT SUPPORT" AND "COMBAT SERVICE SUPPORT" VEHICLES IS JUST AS INTERESTING AS THAT OF THE MAIN BATTLE TANKS. THE RUSSIANS PIONEERED MANY OF THESE VEHICLES, SOME OF WHICH THEN "INSPIRED" AMERICAN DESIGNERS TO PRODUCE SIMILAR SYSTEMS.

MANY OF THE VEHICLES PICTURED IN THIS SECTION ARE OWNED BY PRIVATE COLLECTORS. ALTHOUGH FEW PEOPLE HAVE THE RESOURCES TO PURCHASE AND MAINTAIN MAIN BATTLE TANKS OF ANY VINTAGE, MANY DO MANAGE TO ACQUIRE LIGHTER ARMOR. FOR INSTANCE, A NEIGHBOR, JOE CARDOZA, KEEPS HIS BRITISH SCORPION (FRESH OUT OF MILITARY SERVICE) IN HIS SUBURBAN GARAGE AND HIS WWII CANADIAN BREN CARRIER PARKED IN THE DRIVE. OTHER LOCAL COLLECTORS OWN AND DISPLAY JEEPS FROM THE 1940s TO THE 1970s, AS WELL AS MILITARY TRUCKS FROM SEVERAL NATIONS.

LEFT: An M3 half-track from World War II, beautifully restored. OPPOSITE: The British Saladin wheeled reconnaissance vehicle served long and well around the world in the years following World War II. Its armor will protect its crowded crew from small-arms fire and artillery splinters, but not much more.

07 CC 38

CHAPTER FOURTEEN

SP GUNS AND ARTILLERY

MLRS

Artillery is supposed to be the battlefield's greatest killer, and one of the most efficient killing systems around is the Multiple Launch Rocket System (MLRS). This system was the product of a large international consortium, with members in Britain, the United States, Germany, France, and Italy.

MLRS uses an M2 Bradley hull, chassis, and power train as the foundation for a large rocket launcher. The rockets themselves are 9 inches (22.8cm) in diameter and 11 feet (3.3m) long, and weigh 676 pounds (306.9kg) each. These are free-flight weapons (not guided missiles)–"fire and forget" devices with a maximum range of about 20 miles (32.1km).

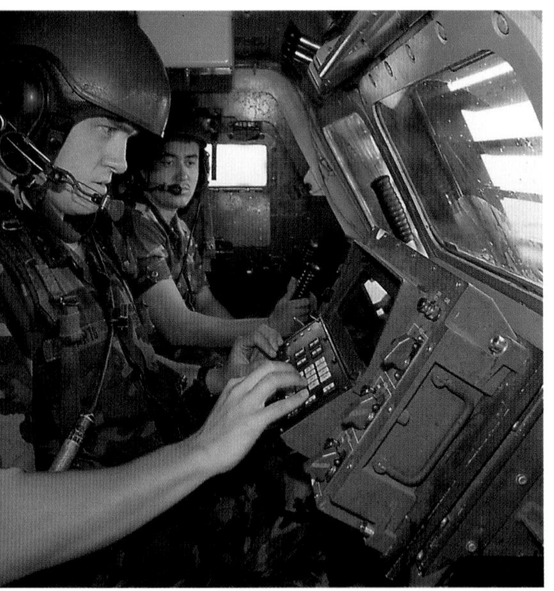

ABOVE: Using information provided over a secure data link, the MLRS crew program the firing computer for a mission.
RIGHT: The commander of this MLRS directs the driver as they maneuver into a firing position.

The basic, plain vanilla payload is the M26 warhead. This weapon fires 644 M77 Dual Purpose Improved Conventional Munitions (DPICMs)–small "submunitions," or bomblets. About the size of a small hand grenade, each is a miniature "shaped charge" that detonates on contact and sends a sharply focused jet of extremely hot gas straight downward. That gas can cut through the top armor of modern tanks. If it lands on the ground, it will spray rocks and casing fragments across a wide area.

Over the target, small explosive linear charges fire and the warhead breaks open, scattering the DPICMs across a broad area. The munitions fall to earth, oriented in flight by a little ribbon drag chute. The result is a dramatic fireworks show. The munitions drop to the target and detonate in a five-second-long shower of sparks, fire, smoke, and destruction. The warhead is programmed to split open about 1,200 feet (365.7m) above the surface, spewing the DPICMs across an area several hundred yards on a side, saturating it with bomblets. Any tanks, trucks, or troops in the area stand a good chance of feeling the effect of one of these munitions, each of which can cut through up to about 4 inches (10.1cm) of armor. That is far thicker than any modern MBT's roof. These submunitions can be defeated by "reactive armor," blocks of explosives arrayed on the outer surface of the armor. HE and similar "chemical

energy" rounds trigger these blocks; when they detonate, the force of the incoming round is deflected. However, reactive armor is useless against kinetic energy projectiles.

The hull and tracks are essentially those of the American M2 Bradley Armored Fighting Vehicle (AFV), but longer. The vehicle is about 21 feet (6.4m) long, while the Bradley is about 5 feet (1.5m) shorter. It is powered by a 500-hp Cummins 8-cylinder turbo-charged diesel linked to a General Electric hydromechanical transmission. The Bradley was designed to keep up with the fast Abrams–and MLRS would, too. Maximum speed is 40 mph (64.3kph). Even with all those rockets on the back, it can still negotiate a 60-degree slope and 40 percent side slope,

LEFT: **Spent rocket packs can be reloaded by the crew using a built-in crane. One man can do it alone if necessary. RIGHT: On the way! The rockets aren't guided but are of free-flight type. Even so, they are quite accurate out to about 9 miles (14.4km). Each warhead contains 644 submunitions, any one of which can kill any modern tank if it lands on vulnerable top-surface armor.**

climb a 3-foot (91.4cm) wall, and cross a 7-foot (2.1m) trench.

Rocket launchers have been around for a long time. The MLRS is a special example of the breed because of its precise navigation and targeting computer systems. The MLRS crew use GPS to precisely establish their firing location. They combine that with firing data from the battery Fire Control Center, which is transmitted over a secure data link. All these elements, and more, are essential to precision fire, and they are integrated automatically in the MLRS computer. The crew launch the rockets from inside the armored cab, then scoot away before the enemy's counter-battery fire starts falling on their position. Both firing and reloading the big rockets can, if necessary, be done by just one crewman.

MLRS was battle tested during Desert Storm/Sabre and did extremely well. As a result, export sales of the system have been very good. More than one thousand launchers have

SPECIFICATIONS	Multiple Launch Rocket System
Crew	3
Weight	55,487 lbs (25.2t) (combat loaded)
Length	22 ft 8 in (6.9m)
Height	8 ft 6 in (2.5m)
Width	10 ft (3m)
Ground clearance	1 ft 4 in (40.6cm)
Ground pressure	14.2 lbs (5.8 kg)
Propulsion	500-hp Cummins VTA-903 8-cylinder turbo-charged diesel
Transmission	General Electric HMPT-500 hydro-mechanical
Speed	40 mph, (64.3kph) 24 mph (38.6kph) cross-country
Range	302 miles (485.9km)
Obstacle crossing	Vertical: 3 ft (91.4cm) Trench: 7 ft (2.1m)
Main armament	12 M77 227mm diameter free-flight rockets with M26 warhead; warhead contains 644 DPICM scatterable submunitions

been ordered, along with 750,000 rockets. The system is currently in service in Britain, France, Germany, Italy, the U.S., Japan, Saudi Arabia, Turkey, and the Netherlands.

FV 433 ABBOT (UK)

Until recently, when it was displaced by the new AS 90, the Abbot was the reliable hired gun for British ground forces. It is a large, self-propelled artillery system able to accurately hit targets about 9 miles (14.4km) away. It was normally found in the 1st Close Support Regiments of the Royal Artillery and used against everything except heavy armor, against which the 105mm round would be ineffective.

The Fv 433 is an AFV 430 series hull and power pack, mated with a 105mm gun, and served by a crew of four. The gun is basically the same system used in the British light-towed 105mm artillery weapon. It is a good gun, but smaller and lighter than the conventional 155mm weapon normally found on modern SP systems.

The Fv 433 Abbot's history goes back before World War II. The British army first experimented with SP artillery in 1927. The concept of making heavy artillery as quick and responsive as the tanks themselves was proven viable while battling fascists in North Africa.

The Abbot's design work began in the late 1950s. A prototype was produced in 1961. Production of the SP gun was awarded to Vickers, and 146 standard vehicles were built for the

British Army, sixty-eight modified models for the Indian Army, and another twenty of the modified version for the British Royal Artillery.

The fairly compact Abbot is 19 feet (5.7m) long, 8 feet 8 inches (2.6m) wide, and about 8 feet (2.4m) high. It weighs 36,500 pounds (16,571kg), combat loaded. It cruises up to 30 mph (48.2kph) on the road, and can swim open expanses of water at about 3 mph (4.8kph). Standard models have a fording screen stowed at the top of the hull, which can be erected in about fifteen minutes, allowing the vehicle to swim rivers and open water. It can climb an obstacle 2 feet (61cm) high and cross a ditch 6 feet 9 inches (2m) wide. Combat range is 242 miles (389.3km).

The vehicle is powered by a Rolls-Royce K60 Mk 4G 6-cylinder multifuel engine producing 240 hp or a K60 Mk 60G diesel generating 213 hp. The transmission is an automatic with six forward and two reverse gears.

The Abbot's main gun is a Royal Armament and Research Establishment–designed 105mm Model L13A1, with fume extractor and double muzzle break. The gun can elevate to +70 degrees, can depress to -5 degrees, and has full 360-degree traverse. Maximum range is 15,500 yards (14,173.2m), or about 9 miles (14.4km). Turret traverse was powered, but elevation and traverse of the gun were manual.

The gun fires a wide range of ammunition types: high-explosive squash-head rounds (HESH) for use against armor; HE against troops, vehicles, and general targets; illumination rounds to light up the nocturnal battlefield; smoke rounds to obscure it by day; and practice rounds. Forty rounds of ammunition for the main gun are carried on the Abbot. Much more is readily available from its faithful squire, the Stalwart resupply vehicle.

The gun is loaded in two phases. First the projectile is loaded in the feed tray and rammed into the breech with an electrical rammer. Then the propellant cartridge case is loaded by hand, and the breech closed.

ABOVE: Turret interior, 105mm Abbot self-propelled gun. LEFT: 105mm projectiles in the ready-racks of the Abbot. Other nations use 120mm or larger weapons for self-propelled guns, so the Abbot is a bit under-gunned for its mission–one reason why it has recently been retired from service. OPPOSITE: A fine example of the Fv 433 Abbot SP gun, owned by Alan Cors.

Abbot's primary role has been with the British Army of the Rhine (BAOR), part of the NATO forces arrayed against the Warsaw Pact during the cold war. Each Royal Artillery regiment included three batteries of six Abbots, a total of 18 Fv 433 SP 105mm guns. Abbot has been, during its career, a well-regarded, agile, and efficient self-propelled gun, even though its 105mm round is less powerful than those used by other nations' forces.

JAGDPANZER 38(T) HETZER TANK DESTROYER

The German Hetzer was a good example of what was once a common breed during World War II—the tank destroyer. In the war's early years, the idea that "the best way to kill a tank was with another tank" still hadn't been accepted by most armor planners. Tanks were thought to be best eliminated with specialized artillery. Therefore, the U.S. went to war with a fleet of towed, high-velocity, flat-shooting 37mm anti-tank guns.

Then the artillery was installed in a tank hull for mobility and protection. The crews of these little towed guns were easy, exposed targets for anybody in range—small arms, artillery, and tankfire tended to shred them all. As an alternative, American, German, and Russian anti-tank guns were soon provided with their own chassis and drivetrain, plus just enough armor to keep out the rain and small-arms fire, and enough frontal armor to defeat some main tank rounds. The resulting vehicle was called a tank destroyer (TD), but it was no more than a self-propelled high-velocity artillery piece. TDs lacked turrets and were very vulnerable from the flanks or rear, but were much more effective than the old towed guns.

The U.S. fielded nearly as many tank destroyer battalions as conventional tanks, and they were busy but not too successful. By the end of the war, with bigger guns and more experience, the concept and the TD battalions were eliminated.

RIGHT: A GI inspects a very dead Hetzer, his hand resting on armor blown apart by internal explosions. The Hetzer was a formidable anti-tank weapon if it could ambush its prey, but very vulnerable to any attack from the rear, and this one seems to have been bushwhacked. BELOW: Hetzer gunner's station and controls. The gun's limited traverse meant that the whole vehicle had to be repositioned unless the target was squarely in the front.

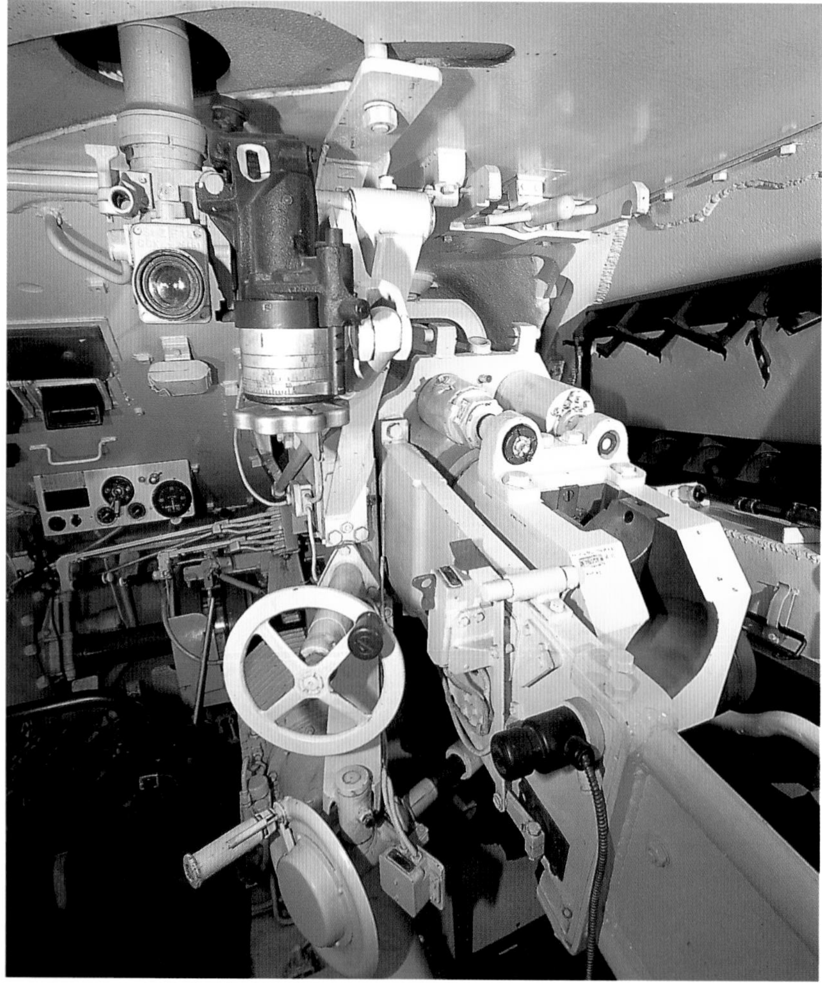

RIGHT: It looks tougher than it is–the armor on the Hetzer is quite thin and the gun's traverse is very restricted. This one is another tank in Jacques Littlefield's extensive collection.

Nearly twenty-six thousand Hetzers were built by the Skoda firm for the German Army during 1944 and 1945. A good gun on a good chassis, it had a little armor protection and a reliable engine, and was not easily visible. It was compact, low, and could tuck itself into the woodwork, ready to ambush a column of Shermans or T-34s rolling around the corner.

If, however, that column decided to sneak around the hill and not blunder into the ambush, the Hetzer crew had a problem. That was because the Hetzer had no turret. The whole vehicle had to be oriented in the general direction of the target. There was no chance of engaging moving targets or dealing with emergencies. The Hetzer had to throw a "sucker punch" and then make a run for the exit. They entered service in May 1944 and served until the end of the war in Europe a year later.

Unlike most armored vehicles, you mount the Hetzer from the rear. Then you clamber across a slippery back deck to the loader's hatch in the middle of the vehicle. You lower yourself in, stepping first on the breech shield of the gun and then the loader's seat.

The Hetzer's main gun bisected the turret. It was a 75mm PaK 39 L/48, with very limited elevation and traverse. The gunner sat to the left of the breech, right behind the driver. The loader sat behind him. All around the turret interior are racks for ammunition. When the vehicle was combat loaded and crewed up, it got crowded.

The Hetzer's secondary armament is a single MG 34 7.62mm machine gun with a drum magazine. This weapon can be operated remotely, from inside the turret, through the use of a periscopic sight. When that drum ran out or the gun jammed, though, some lucky volunteer had to pop outside to reload or clear the weapon.

A 150-hp 6-cylinder water-cooled engine propels the Hetzer. It is a noisy engine, at least for the crew. The dri-

ver has two little vision blocks and no hatch, so he can't drive unbuttoned. His controls are conventional lateral levers. Typical of the period, they require a lot of muscle power.

The Hetzer doesn't offer much in the way of crew protection, even at the front of the vehicle. The side armor is only ¼ inch (6mm) thick, far thinner than that of any tank, and the front glacis plate is only 2⅓ inches (5.9cm) thick. That armor is steeply angled, however, which greatly increases its effectiveness.

The Hetzer was such a good design that, like many other German designs, it lived on after the war, soldiering for other nations. Switzerland upgraded the vehicle with 160-hp engines and continued to use them into the 1960s.

CHAPTER FIFTEEN

APCs: ARMORED PERSONNEL CARRIERS

SAXON

GKN Defence's Saxon is a good modern example of a wheeled armored personnel carrier, currently serving with the British Army. Unlike the U.S. tradition of using tracked vehicles for this chore, British forces have long utilized wheeled versions, and with great success. And these APCs on tires have gotten a real workout. They've seen action in places like Northern Ireland, where the citizens provided a realistic training environment by throwing bricks, rocks, petrol bombs, and grenades at British Army patrols.

As with most APCs, including the M113 and BMP, the Saxon is a multirole vehicle, customized to do all sorts of chores. The plain vanilla version seats up to ten troops with combat equipment. The same vehicle can be tricked out as a command version, with map tables, too many radios—and most likely a coffeepot. It can also be customized into a repair-and-recovery vehicle with a huge winch, a mortar carrier, or a recon vehicle for surveillance and observation missions.

The AT105 Saxon is a current-generation combat vehicle, still in its prime. The first prototype appeared in 1975, the first production versions a year later. The name was applied in 1982. Most are powered by a 164-hp Bedford 500-series 6-cylinder diesel, coupled to an Allison Transmission AT-545 automatic gearbox with four forward gears and one reverse. A 195-hp Perkins and a 160-hp Cummins 6BT 5.91-liter engine are available as options. The Saxon motors up to 60 mph (96.5kph) on the highway. With a full tank (38 gallons [143.8L]of fuel), the vehicle has a 288-mile (463.3km) road range.

Saxons have a few quirks. One is an optional set of "run-flat" tires, which could get shot full of holes and still get you out of Dodge. As with many contemporary armored vehicles, the Saxon uses a 24-volt electrical system, instead of the typical 12-volt system used on civilian and some military vehicles.

OPPOSITE: British armored support vehicles are designed to wring many missions from a single basic design, particularly so with the Saxon. This one is tricked out as an ambulance, but many other variants are offered by GKN Defence. BELOW: A pair of Saxon APCs, each accommodating up to ten fully kitted-up "squaddies." These vehicles have gotten a real workout in Northern Ireland.

About seven hundred Saxons have been sold to date, most to the British Army and others to Hong Kong, Kuwait, Nigeria, Oman, the United Arab Emirates, and elsewhere.

Saxon Patrol variants began replacing the Humber for patrol work in Northern Ireland in 1992. This version uses the Cummins diesel, automatic transmission, and either 2- or 4-wheel drive. The Saxon Patrol also has a barricade removal device, searchlights, bulletproof glass with wire screens, and other enhancements. The Saxon may not be the most muscular or handsome vehicle on the battlefield, but it has proved to be highly efficient and effective.

BMP-1 AND BMP-2 INFANTRY FIGHTING VEHICLES

Among the most radical and impressive Soviet combat vehicles produced during the cold war was the Boevaya

LEFT: Early Soviet BMP-1s parade in Moscow's Red Square. The BMP is a low, agile, heavily armed personnel carrier and fighting vehicle, the inspiration for many Western combat vehicles like the Bradley. That's a Sagger wire-guided anti-tank missile mounted on the low-velocity 73mm cannon.

Mashina Pekhota, or BMP, an innovative APC that first appeared in Red Square in 1967.

Actually, the BMP is more than just an APC. It was the very first of the Mechanized Infantry Combat Vehicles (MICV) and the inspiration for many others–including the American M2 Bradley.

At first glance, the BMP looks fast, sleek, and lethal. Looks are not deceiving, for the BMP proved to be all of the above. The BMP quickly became a standard item of equipment within Warsaw Pact forces. It continues to serve more than a dozen armies. It has been an export market success story for its designers and current builder of the BMP-2, the Kurgan Machine Construction Plant.

It is a fast, light, versatile vehicle, full of interesting features. Unlike the U.S. M113, the troops in the BMP can fight from under armor through ingenious ports for their AKMS rifles and PKM 7.62mm machine gun. The vehicle mounts a diminutive yet effective cannon. Troops can actually fire their personal weapons through ports in the side of the vehicle. BMPs are normally set up to fire a Sagger wire-guided anti-tank missile, too, so it is a potent package.

BMPs carry eight fully equipped troops in relative discomfort, back to back. Twin doors at the rear of the vehicle, with vision and firing ports in each, provide access to the battlefield when it is time to get out.

BMP BASICS

The BMP is 20 feet 8 inches (6.3m) long, 10 feet (3m) wide, and an amazing 6 feet (1.8m) high. That low profile allows the vehicle to slither into all kinds of little hiding places and low spots in the terrain, with just its turret peeking over the top. Of course the downside to that low profile is that the troops are crammed into the rear compartment, and there isn't much room for expansion. The U.S. M113 is more

OPPOSITE: A platoon of BMPs assigned to a mechanized rifle regiment train in the Ural mountains during the cold years of the Cold War.

than 2 feet (61cm) taller, but that extra space allows the troops more room, and it allows the vehicle to function as a command track–a mobile headquarters component of the Tactical Operations Center (TOC).

The hull is welded steel, with a steeply angled glacis plate. Maximum armor thickness is about ½ inch (1.2cm), enough to stop heavy machine-gun fire and artillery fragments. It is water-tight and could swim without preparation.

A 280-hp 6-cylinder in-line water-cooled diesel engine powers the BMP. The power plant is installed in the front of the vehicle, to the right of the driver. Maximum speed is 36 mph (57.9kph) on the road, much less across country, and about 3 mph (4.8kph) in the water.

BMP CREW

The BMP holds a three-man crew: driver, gunner, and commander. The driver sits at the left front of the hull, the commander behind him, and the gunner in the turret in the center of the vehicle.

The driver can operate the vehicle either from an open hatch or buttoned up. When under armor, he has three periscopes to watch the terrain ahead. The center scope is removable and can be replaced with a much taller version for amphibious operations when the trim vane (a panel on the front of the vehicle) would otherwise block his line of sight. The driver also has an IR driving light, installed on the right front of the BMP, and an IR night-vision device. The driver's controls include all the normal engine management instruments and switches, plus controls for the pneumatic engine starter. He can also clean the commander's and his own vision systems with a remote system that sprays cleaning fluid and high-pressure air on the front surfaces, blasting off mud and dust.

The commander sits behind the driver, to the left of the turret and gunner's station. From this perch, the commander can both keep an eye on his passengers and offer his crew helpful advice, wit, and wisdom while he does his best to keep the vehicle on station with the rest of the assault.

The gunner has the best seat in the house. He sits in a little one-man turret with 360-degree traverse, a 73mm Model 2A28 smoothbore weapon that feeds from a forty-round magazine, and a 7.62mm PKT co-ax machine gun.

There are three viewing systems in the turret: a monocular periscope on the left with a 15-degree field of view and 6X magnification in daylight mode, and 6.7X and 6-degree angle of view in low-light mode. Night engagements with this "starlight scope" system are limited to about

SPECIFICATIONS	BMP-3 Infantry Fighting Vehicle
Crew	3, plus 7 infantry
Weight	41,189 lbs (18,700kg)
Length with gun forward	23 ft 7⅞ in (7.2 m)
Turret height	7 ft 6½ in (2.3 m)
Width	10 ft 7⅛ in (3.23 m)
Ground clearance	18 in (45.7cm)
Ground pressure	8.5 lbs (3.9 kg)
Propulsion	UTD-29M 10-cylinder diesel generating 500-hp
Transmission	hydromechanical; four forward, two reverse gears
Speed	70 kph on road, 10 kph in water
Range	375 miles (603.3km)
Obstacle crossing	Vertical: 2 ft 8 in (81.2cm) Trench: 7 ft (2.1m)
Main armament	100mm gun/missile
Co-axial weapon	30mm cannon

975 yards (891.5m). The sight itself incorporates a stadiametric range-finding system, a heater that keeps it from fogging up, and a little windshield wiper that keeps the outside of the optics clear.

The 73mm smoothbore 2A28 gun is a combination gun and rocket launcher that fires a variety of HEAT and HE-FRAG rounds as far as 1,400 yards (1,280.1m). Those rounds aren't propelled all the way to the target by conventional combustion chamber pressure; the gun only gets the round started. The HEAT round leaves the muzzle at about 1,400 fps (426.7mps), then accelerates to 2,300 feet per second (701mps) after a PG-9V rocket motor on the projectile fires. About the same time, fins pop out of the round, providing some stability, and the weapon zooms downrange.

RIGHT: Alan Cors' handsome BMP. Loaded with innovations and brilliantly designed for battle, the BMP is an impressive combat vehicle in many ways. BELOW: Soviet infantry bail out of their battlefield taxi in this carefully staged photograph from TASS. In combat they might be glad to go–those doors are full of fuel, and a .50cal incendiary hit would easily set fire to the BMP and its passengers.

The warhead can blast through about 12 inches (30.4cm) of conventional steel armor at 0 degrees incidence, enough to defeat many MBTs, if the BMP can get in a quartering or rear shot. The problem, though, is that the BMP's range is far shorter than a tank's–the likelihood of getting in a "sucker punch" on such an adversary is poor, with unhappy results in the event of failure.

Besides the 73mm weapon, the gunner has a co-ax 7.62mm machine gun for dealing with enemy dismounts. This is effective as an "area" weapon to about 1,700 feet (518.1m). It is fed by a continuous two-thousand-round belt. If the gunner isn't careful with his rate of fire–a problem in combat–the barrel will start glowing bright red, and rounds will "cook off," as the heat ignites the propellant, before he pulls the trigger.

Mounting rails for a AT-3 Sagger wire-guided anti-tank missile are attached to the 73mm gun's barrel. The Sagger has about a 3,300-yard (3,017.5m) range and was very effective in its 1973 combat debut by the Egyptians and the Syrians against the Israelis–much to the surprise of the Israelis. Using a small box and a video game–like joystick, the commander

"flies" the missile out to the target. When the Sagger wants to stay hidden, it can also be launched from a remote mount by use of a 270-foot (82.2m) cable and launcher.

There were problems with the Sagger: it was slow; if the wires were cut, the missile lost control; it was strictly a daylight system; sixty seconds were required for a reload—and a minute was a long time with the commander or one of his associates exposed to the elements; and a fresh missile could not be mounted until the first one had hit (or missed) its target. Most of these problems remain today, but a new version with an IR seeker is expected to improve long-range and nighttime performance.

Five Sagger missiles are typically issued for combat operations—one on the rail and four in the vehicle. Two of those are ready-rounds in the commander's turret. Another two are stowed in the hull.

In the troop compartment, all eight passengers have a periscope to observe the battlefield, and below that is a special adapter for the AK assault rifle. Each of the periscopes is heated to keep them from fogging up in cold weather. The forward weapon stations are supplied with PKM machine guns, while the other three on each side have AKMS 7.62mm weapons. Both types are specially adapted to the BMP and its firing ports. The normal AK47 or AK74 won't fit. While you can't aim the weapon from inside, a squad can certainly lay down a large volume of well-directed area suppression fire. With all eight of those weapons blasting away, the interior will quickly fill up with fumes. To prevent this, the BMP has a hose and cowling for each weapon, coupled to a vacuum pump to extract the smoke.

Hatches above the crew compartment allow the troops to stand up to fight, or enjoy the ride. They can engage foolish aircraft that loitered within range of their small arms or Grail shoulder-launched anti-aircraft missiles (often stowed aboard).

Come bail-out time, the BMP's passengers peek out the vision

RIGHT: Caught by American ground-attack aircraft on a road in Normandy, this German SdKfz 251 is a smoking wreck. But the design was a sound one that outlived World War II to serve several nations.

blocks in each of the two doors at the rear of the vehicle. They then abandon ship and make a run for it. Since both doors also serve as fuel tanks–and are quite vulnerable to puncture wounds, and consequent fire–the troops are glad to go.

BMPS FOR THE FUTURE

An improved version of the BMP, the BMP-2 Infantry Fighting Vehicle (IFV), appeared in 1982, with thicker armor, a bigger and better 30mm gun, and a seat for the commander in the turret. More than twenty thousand of these are in service today, most with the usual suspects from the cold war days. A few are owned by Iraq and Iran–those not yet destroyed by Gulf wars and skirmishes.

The BMP-3 arrived in 1990, with the same basic foundation as the BMP-1 and -2, but with a much-enhanced weapon suite. These weapons are part of a system designated 2K23. They are all mounted in a bigger turret, and include a 100mm gun, 30mm cannon, and 7.62mm co-ax machine gun. This new BMP has a 500-hp engine and 5-speed hydro-mechanical transmission.

The gun fires HE-FRAG rounds or laser-guided missiles effective to around 4,400 yards (4,023.3m). It is aimed with a fully stabilized day/night sight system. The TC and gunner both have controls for the turret and gun, and can elevate the gun up to 60 degrees for engagements against helicopters.

The new 30mm cannon uses a simplified design to improve reliability, but offers automatic dual ammunition feed. Choice of rounds include armor-piercing-incendiary (API), high-explosive-incendiary (HEI), or high-explosive-tracer (HET), at a cyclic rate of fire of 330 rounds per second. Each of these rounds has a muzzle velocity of about 3,300 fps (1,005.8mps) and is effective against light armor out to just over a mile (1.6km), and helicopters out to over 2 miles (3.2km).

The weapon system includes a ballistic computer and laser range finder, both of which contribute to a high degree of accuracy. The BMP-3 can engage a target at 1,100 yards (1,005.8m) in just three seconds with a 90 percent "probability of kill" (PK). A second target can be engaged 4.9 seconds after the first.

SDKFZ 251

German land combat doctrine during the late 1930s called for close cooperation between infantry and armor. This concept of operations has been adopted by all major armies and is still accepted today. Infantry–popping up from holes and from behind trees and rocks with PIATs (British weapons–it

stands for projector, infantry, anti-tank) and bazookas (American infantry anti-tank weapons), grenades, and satchel charges—are the tank's worst enemy. The best weapon to use against anti-tank infantry is infantry of your own, cleaning out ambush sites and engaging enemy dismounts hidden in places a tank can't go.

ABOVE: SdKfz 251 from Alan Cors' fleet of military vehicles. RIGHT: Here's a counterfeit SdKfz 251, actually a postwar Czech variant masquerading as the genuine item during a World War II reenactment in Britain.

Tanks and infantry worked together from the beginning. The idea, at least initially, was for the tank to slow down and keep pace with the foot soldiers. That was still SOP in the U.S. and Britain at the start of World War II. Then the Germans decided to speed things up. They quickened the pace of some infantry to keep pace with the armor, about 15 mph (24.1kph) on roads and almost as fast across good open terrain. The Germans instantly transformed land warfare with their new stunning speed. *Blitzkrieg!*

Fundamental to this kind of assault was a new kind of APC. The German APC was the Mittlerer Schützenpanzerwagen (SdKfz) 251, designed in 1934 and put into service in 1939, just in time for the invasion of Poland.

The SdKfz 251 was a half-track multipurpose vehicle with light armor protection. Crews were safe from small-arms fire and artillery fragments, as long as it didn't come from overhead.

As a troop transport, the SdKfz 251 carried ten soldiers and their weapons and combat equipment. It could carry a variety of other things: anti-aircraft weapons, rocket launchers, large-caliber anti-tank weapons, engineer squads, and more. The SdKfz 251 was so successful that it participated in every major German campaign of the war. It continued in production after the war in Czechoslovakia, and stayed in service with several armies until quite recently. It was certainly the inspiration, if not the model, for the U.S. half-tracks, the M2 series.

The SdKfz 251 was developed in 1934 by the Hanomag company to fulfill a German Army requirement for a 2.95-ton (2.6t) vehicle. The original need was for something suitable for towing artillery, but that was soon

modified to include an armored compartment for infantry. Over the years, that basic foundation has been adapted to more than twenty variants.

The vehicle is 19 feet (5.7m) long, 6 feet 10 inches (2m) wide, and 5 feet 9 inches (1.7m) high. The hood is tilted forward at a steep angle, providing much better visibility for the driver than did the equivalent Allied M3 series. A 100-hp 6-cylinder Maybach gasoline engine provides enough power to get the big APC up to 34 mph (54.7kph) on a level road. With a full tank of gas, the SdKfz 251's range is 200 miles (321.8km).

M3 HALF-TRACK

The M3 was one of many WWII vehicles that—though designed and built in the United States—served with all the Allied nations, in profusion, and in numerous variants. The M3 APC design development began in the late 1930s, when an armored and enlarged White Scout Car had its rear wheels replaced by the track assemblies and drivetrain components from a Mammon-Herrington T9 half-track truck. Originally called the T7, the vehicle was renamed the Half Track Personnel Carrier M3 by the U.S. Army on September 19, 1940.

The M3 and its variants—the M2 Half Track Car and M4 81mm Mortar Carrier—were originally contracted to the Autocar Company. The initial order was for 424 vehicles. Larger orders followed that were far beyond Autocar's production capacity. Contracts were signed with the Diamond T and White Motor companies for more M3s—with provisions that the components would, with the exception of the armor plate, be interchangeable.

The M3 Half Track carries ten soldiers and their combat equipment. Top speed is 45 mph (72.4kph). Range is 210 miles (337.8km). The armor–from ¼ inch to ½ inch (6 to 12mm) thick–protects passengers and the three-man crew from small-arms fire and all but overhead artillery fragments. The vehicle is armed with the usual .50cal heavy machine gun, an effective weapon against other thin-skinned vehicles and aircraft. It is 20 feet 3 inches (6.1m) long, 7 feet 4 inches (2.2m) wide, and 7 feet 5 inches (2.3m) high. It weighes 10 tons (9,080kg) combat loaded, and is powered by a strong and reliable 147-hp White 6-cylinder engine.

Half-tracks served by the tens of thousands during World War II, as well as in the postwar era. One variant, the M16A1, boasts four .50cal machine guns in a powered mount, a very potent piece of equipment for use against low-flying aircraft and ground targets. It was extremely effective in Korea, where it mowed down the human-wave assaults by the North Korean and Chinese armies.

The U.S. Army discarded half-tracks in the 1950s in favor of fully tracked APCs, but the Israelis continued to use them extensively during

OPPOSITE: A M2A1 rumbles along a sandy desert trail during training in the California Mojave desert in 1942. **LEFT:** Jacques Littlefield's factory-fresh M3 towing a 75mm anti-tank gun. **BELOW:** Soviet Marines drive their BTR-60P ashore from their huge amphibious assault ship.

their 1967 and 1973 wars, and still have some in service. M3s also serve South Korea, Taiwan, and Uruguay.

BTR-60

The Russian BTR-60 was one of the most prolific and popular APCs of the cold war. Many are currently in service with nations around the world. While American APCs were usually fully tracked, Russian and many European APCs ride on rubber tires.

There are some real advantages to APCs on tires. They have lower rolling resistance, are easily maintained, and have a simplified drivetrain. They are preferable for urban operations. On good roads, too, they are usually faster than tracked vehicles.

The BTR-60 is intended to rapidly transport a large squad of Soviet soldiers into battle, close behind the assault elements, in just about any kind of terrain. It uses eight driven wheels, the front four of which are steerable. Large hatches at the rear allow the troops to de-bus, but Soviet photos often showed them bailing out through the top and jumping down to the ground in dramatic style.

The BTR-60 is a big APC: 24 feet (7.3m) long and more than 9 feet (2.7m) wide, and weighing about 10 tons (9,080kg). It carries a crew of two plus fourteen combat-equipped infantry under side, but not top, armor. Later versions, starting with the BTR-60PK, are fully enclosed and have NBC protection, both important improvements.

Two 90-hp engines power the BTR-60 to a maximum road speed of

about 50 mph (80.4kph). Road range is 311 miles (500.4km). It is also fully amphibious without preparation and, propelled by a water jet, can go about 6 mph (9.6kph) across open water.

The primary mission for the BTR-60 is with the numerous Russian motorized rifle divisions, rather than with the tank divisions. They use the more combat-ready BMP with its integral anti-armor weapons. The BTR-60 mounts only a single heavy machine gun.

Two major variants of the basic vehicle are the BTR-PU, a command vehicle with radios and map tables, and the BTR-PB, also with additional radios, but designed for use by forward air controllers (FACs). The BTR continues to be a superb armored personnel carrier, adapted to the challenges of the twenty-first century.

ABOVE: A mechanized rifle regiment passes in review, riding BTR-60PBs, during "West 81" exercises. RIGHT: BTR-70s, BTR-60s, and their crews patrol Tskhinvali, South Odessa, Georgia, during January 1991. The rifle regiment's mission was to prevent clashes between ethnic groups in the days following independence from the old Soviet Union.

110

C H A P T E R S I X T E E N

SCOUTS AND RECON

"Scouts out!" is the first command heard by an armor unit preparing an attack. It is heard hours or days before the tank crews mount up and move out. The scouts—whether in their fast, light vehicles, in helicopters, or on foot—gather information on the enemy and terrain ahead, then report back to the commander.

They seek invisibility, disappearing into the woodwork—or the rocky desert. These covert missions require vehicles with speed, stealth, and the ability to occasionally shoot it out when discovered. Scout vehicles are a specialized breed, with an emphasis on speed rather than heavy armor. They are also typically small, the better to hide themselves.

The following are just a few examples of the numerous breed.

FV 101 COMBAT VEHICLE RECON TRACKED—SCORPION

The British Scorpion is a quick-tracked recon vehicle with a very big stinger, a crew of three, and an ability to go just about anywhere. Scorpions have served with the British Army from 1972 to the present. They also served the armies of Belgium, Bolivia, Iran, Ireland, Tanzania, and many other nations. The Scorpion can't do everything, but it does do a lot quite well.

Fv 101 Scorpion is fabricated from sheet aluminum armor. While this armor will not protect against anti-tank weapons, it keeps the three-man crew safe enough from machine-gun fire and most artillery air-burst splinters. That lack of armor translates into very light weight—only about 17,000 pounds (7,718kg) combat loaded. As a result, the Scorpion is easily transportable by air; it can even be air-dropped by parachute. Two can fit in a single C-130 Hercules.

The latest versions of the Fv 101 Scorpion include a laser range finder and thermal imaging sight for its large 76mm L23 gun. Forty rounds of ammunition are carried for the 76mm gun, plus another three thousand rounds for the 7.62mm machine gun. The main gun's range is about 3 miles (4.8km) with HESH ammunition.

An export version is also available with a 90mm gun and Perkins diesel engine. The diesel's excellent fuel economy gives this version a 600-mile (965.4km) range.

With the standard 195-hp 4.2-liter Jaguar gasoline-fueled engine, it can

RIGHT: FV 101 Scorpion of the 16th/5th Queen's Royal Lancers reconnaissance patrol during the Turkish invasion of Cyprus in 1974.

CHALK

go faster than 50 mph (80.4kph) with a range of about 380 miles (611.4km). It can climb an 18-inch (45.7cm) obstacle, cross a 6-foot (1.8m) trench, negotiate a 60 percent grade, and ford to a 3-foot (91.4cm) depth.

SCORPIONS IN THE GULF WAR

Scorpions—operated by the 16th/5th Queen's Royal Lancers (16th/5th L), a recon regiment, and by an additional recon squadron from the Queen's Dragoon Guards (QDG)—went to war in 1991 as part of Britain's contribution to the Gulf War.

While scouting ahead of Brig. Patrick Cordingly's 7th Armoured Brigade, B Squadron, 16th/5th L, and A Squadron QDG made contact with Iraqi armor units at first light on February 26. The enemy units, a mechanized infantry battalion, fired on the Scorpions and were engaged in turn by Royal Artillery batteries, MLRS batteries, A-10 ground attack aircraft, and Swingfire TOW missiles fired by the Scorpions (in Striker variant form) themselves. All four squadrons became involved in this fight, engaging and defeating Iraqi T-55 tanks at long range, with no losses of their own.

THE SCORPION FAMILY

The foundation for the Fv 101 Scorpion was so sound that a whole family of armored vehicles have been designed around it. The others are

OPPOSITE: **Alan Cors' handsome little Scorpion on display for the public. BELOW: Scimitar is a more modern version of the Scorpion, with a high-velocity 30mm Rarden cannon and built almost entirely of aluminum.**

Striker, Spartan, Sultan, and Samaritan.

STRIKER

Striker is an anti-tank platform. It mounts ten Swingfire missiles, each with a maximum effective range of around 2½ miles (4km). The rounds are carried in a "hammer-head" launcher on the deck of the vehicle. They are lowered during travel and then erected to engage targets. Although Striker is lightly armored, its speed allows it to keep up with the fastest modern MBTs and score opportunistic shots on enemy armor.

Striker's main offensive threat is a Swingfire anti-tank guided weapon (ATGW). Five ATGW missiles are housed in a launcher attached to the rear of the upper deck of the vehicle. Another five are stowed inside.

Swingfire is a 60-pound (27.2kg) weapon manufactured by British Aerospace. It can engage targets from 165 yards to more than 2 miles (150.8 to 3.2km). Normally, a crew has to position a launch vehicle for such missiles within line of sight to the target, but this is not the case with the Striker (or the BMP-3). It has a remote controller that gives the crew greater security. The Striker can be hidden entirely behind a berm, in a ditch or depression, or behind a wall. The gunner carries the missile controller to a convenient observation point within about 300 yards (274.3m) of the vehicle and fires the weapon from there.

SPARTAN

Spartan is the APC version of the Scorpion introduced in 1978. With a crew of three, Spartan can deliver four fully equipped (and crowded) soldiers to the battle. These soldiers might comprise a mortar fire control party, a recon team, a missile team, or perhaps an observer/sniper team.

Passengers embark on the Spartan through a hatch at the rear of the vehicle. The infantry has two periscopes, but can't engage targets from within the APC. A ground surveillance radar is sometimes fitted to Spartan's exterior.

SULTAN AND SAMARITAN

Yet another variant of the basic Scorpion chassis is an armored command track called the Sultan. Cramped accommodations for up to six crew are alleged, but they will have to be pretty small and will have to leave most of their kit outside. A tent offers maneuver room for the staff when the vehicle has to be halted for any length of time. The Sultan's hull has provisions for the radio and map boards that are the tools of the trade for a modern commander. Its only weapon is a 7.62mm machine gun.

The good Samaritan is the ambulance version of the Scorpion, with room for four stretcher cases, or five "walking wounded" plus an aide man, the vehicle commander, and the driver. It carries no weapons.

FAST ATTACK VEHICLES

For many years, the major powers of the world focused their planning on a massive conventional- and nuclear-weapon exchange between the WarPac nations and NATO. Instead, they ended up fighting little brushfire wars. For Russia, it was Afghanistan. For England, the Falklands. The United States had Grenada, Panama, and the Persian Gulf. Much of the combat equipment (and training) was inappropriate and inadequate for the actual combat missions. As a result, a major rethinking of combat vehicles was undertaken and the result was very interesting.

Some of these were modern versions of the old gun jeeps from fifty years ago, utility vehicles mounting the biggest weapons the chassis would tolerate. The British have led the way in this category, with vehicles like the Land Rover "Defender" 110 Light Vehicle and the Wessex Sabre Light Strike Vehicle. Similar versions are available from Spain, Portugal, South Africa, Sweden, and France.

The Fast Attack Vehicle (FAV) is a military-issue dune buggy built by Chenowith Racing Products in San Diego, California, primarily for the U.S. Navy's SEALs. This buggy has a nasty attitude—and nasty passengers to match it.

The history of today's U.S. light-strike vehicle goes back more than ten years, all the way to the U.S. Army's old 9th Infantry Division—which routinely received experimental, oddball, and one-off equipment—and was known universally throughout the army at the time as the "Toys-R-Us Division." At one point, the 9th had a

RIGHT: The Wessex Sabre is one of several similar very light recon vehicles designed for speed and stealth. This one is armed with .50cal M2 and 7.62mm machine guns.

COMMANDER GARY STUBBLEFIELD ON THE FAV

All eight FAVs in the current U.S. Navy inventory are "owned" by the U.S. Navy's Special Warfare Command (SPECWARCOM) and assigned to SEAL Team 3, the component of the SEALs who train to operate in the desert. Gary Stubblefield, Commander USN (retired), commanded SEAL Team 3 when the vehicles were just coming into service. Stubblefield observed their teething troubles and first schoolyard fights, and here offers some insights into their use.

The FAV gets mixed reviews from the guys in the SEAL teams. Some say they are nothing but big play toys, and that the guys who use them are going to get hurt in them. And, of course, we had an almost-fatal accident with one early in the program when a gun swung around and hit a guy in the head. But we had great success with them in Desert Storm. The FAVs got way out across the lines, patrolled aggressively, and were the first vehicles into Kuwait City.

Team 3 used them for two roles: cross-border recon, and standby for downed-pilot recovery. Although they didn't actually get to rescue any pilots, they were always considered one of the best resources available for the job, and were often on call for that mission.

The standard procedure for using the FAVs is to always send them out in pairs, just as we do with combat swimmers. That way, if something goes wrong, one vehicle can provide support for the other, and, if necessary, tow a breakdown back in or at least rescue the crew.

One common task for them is to set up listening posts. You do that by finding a spot out in the enemy-controlled area suitable for overwatch and interdiction, then you find a place to hide and camouflage the vehicles. Then you wait and watch and listen—and report back. Sometimes, in the Gulf, these guys would go way out there. For those missions, they rigged auxiliary fuel tanks for longer-range operations. They also rigged litters on the sides of the vehicle for evacuating injured pilots, if necessary.

Obviously, you can't slug it out with enemy armor using an FAV, but you certainly can use it to ambush tanks. Since they're fast and maneuverable—and you can get them into places where armor is likely to bog down—the vehicle is well suited to engage armor with the AT-4 missiles, or with command-detonated mines, from relative safety.

Since Desert Storm, the FAVs have been well respected by most of the guys in the teams—and the planners and commanders, too. While there doesn't seem to be any interest right now in adding any more to the existing inventory of eight vehicles, Team 3 is still using them in the Middle East and is happy with their performance. SPECWARCOM is still working on some details of the vehicle—lowering the radar signature and exhaust noise, for example. They've been highly effective and have worked pretty much as advertised.

dune buggy of its own. It seemed effective for recon and light-strike missions, but never got past the test-and-evaluation phase. It was a good idea, though, and was resurrected when the Army and Navy started looking for vehicles for their "sneaky Petes," the special operators of the Army's Green Berets and Navy SEALs. Chenowith's primary business is the construction of off-road racing vehicles, which dominate the Baja 1000 race. The FAV took that racing design and brought it up to MilSpec standards—with some added extras.

The FAV is a tiny, feather-light off-road vehicle designed for recon and light-strike missions, primarily in the desert. It is suitable for some kinds of rescue operations, such as scooping a solo pilot up after he's ejected behind enemy lines and before the opposition finds him. If that pilot is part of an aircraft crew, however, somebody is going to be very uncomfortable—there wasn't room for more than three people on the FAV.

But there is room for a nice variety of weapons. The FAV comes with a TOW missile launcher, a recoilless rifle, and a 30mm Chain Gun or 40mm Mark 19 Grenade Launcher. These crew-served weapons are

mounted on the roll bar, and provide slight protection for the crew. There is no armor. Speed and agility are the only protection the FAV crews have to escape from trouble.

Power is provided by an air-cooled STD 94-hp gasoline engine. The power plant is linked to a sturdy manual transmission with four forward gears and one reverse. Since the vehicle weighs only about 2,100 pounds (953.4kg), that power-to-weight ratio makes the FAV a land rocket. It can go faster than 85 mph (136.7kph), and accelerates from 0 to 30 mph (48.2kph) in a head-snapping 3.6 seconds. Its four-wheel independent suspension smoothes out some of the bumps, and the low center of gravity helps keep it from rolling over during those high-speed evasive maneuvers. It is twice as fast as an HMMWV over open terrain.

At first glance, the FAV seemed like a battlefield weakling. Then the Department of Defense tested the vehicle against an M1A1 in a game of "laser tag" at the National Training Center (NTC)–a vast expanse of desert in California's Mojave Desert–and the FAV beat the Abrams three times out of four.

FAVS IN THE GULF WAR

Both the U.S. Navy SEALs and U.S. Marine Corps Force Recon teams used Scorpions during Desert Shield/Desert Storm, with excellent results in both cases.

ABOVE: U.S. Navy SEALs have their own little dune buggy, the Fast Attack Vehicle. This one is loaded for bear with a .50cal heavy machine gun and a couple of bunker-busting and anti-armor AT-4 rocket launchers.

The SEALs had them first. Scorpions were airlifted in during the summer buildup, and the SEALs patrolled aggressively with them. Marines got another eight FAVs in early January, shortly before the start of the ground war.

One of the primary missions for the FAV in the Gulf was "deep reconnaissance and covert surveillance," missions conducted aggressively by

OPPOSITE: The Brits call it the Warrior and it is a vehicle that lives up to its name. This one is fitted up with a 30mm RARDEN cannon in a turret with 360-degree rotation. The "squaddie" would normally not take up such a position, but this is a publicity photo.

British SAS, U.S. Army Green Berets, and U.S. Navy SEALs before and during the ground combat phase of operations. Reportedly, this included using laser-designators to "mark" or "paint" Iraqi targets, such as mobile SCUD launchers, for aircraft equipped with so-called smart laser-guided bombs.

Another important mission for the FAV in the Gulf was scouting and flank security. Normally, this was supposed to be done by the Hummers but, during the Gulf War, M1A1s and Bradleys outran their HMMWV security elements. The Hummers couldn't keep pace. The FAVs could go twice as fast as the Hummers over broken ground–and on the highway, too–so they were sometimes used to support the armor. A much more common application for the FAV, however, was to patrol around high-value targets, like airports.

Because of their small size and great speed, the FAVs were used "on point" to spearhead the attack of Task Force "Ripper" up into eastern Kuwait. An FAV was the first coalition vehicle into Kuwait City and appeared on the cover of *Newsweek* magazine–complete with a crew of SEALs ordering the photographer not to take their picture.

They were sent on long patrols into Kuwait and Iraq, sometimes on missions lasting four days and covering 650 miles (1,045.8km).

SPECIFICATIONS	**Chenowith Fast Attack Vehicle**
Crew	2 or 3
Weight	2,100 lbs (.95t); 3,700 lbs (1.68t) gross with max payload
Length	13 ft 5 in (4m)
Height	6 ft 7 in (2m)
Width	6 ft 11 in (2.1m)
Ground clearance	16 in (40.6cm)
Ground pressure	13.7 lbs (6.2kg)
Propulsion	Modified 2000cc air-cooled 4-cylinder Volkswagen gasoline engine generating 120 hp at 4500 rpm
Transmission	4-speed syncromesh
Speed	+85 mph (+136.7kph)
Acceleration	0 to 30 mph (48.2km) in 3.6 seconds
Range	320 miles (514.8km) with standard tank; 600 miles (965.4km) with optional long-range tanks
Standard weapons	.50cal M2 machine gun, 2 AT-4 anti-tank rockets
Optional weapons	Mk 19 40mm Grenade Launcher, Low-Recoil 30mm cannon, M60 7.62mm machine gun, TOW-2 anti-tank missile
NBC protection	The power of prayer

WARRIOR

Another star performer from Britain is the Warrior APC/Armored Fighting Vehicle (AFV) and its excellent 30mm RARDEN cannon. Actually, Warrior is part of a large family of variants. Some have no cannon at all; others had missiles and many other options. Warrior replaced the FV432, a 1960s APC that had reached the end of its service life. The program for Warrior began in 1980. The first prototypes arrived in 1984.

The basic Warrior is similar in appearance and mission to both the American M2 Bradley and Russian BMP. All are "fighting vehicles" rather than "battlefield taxis," like the old M113. They are all fast, low, and

armed with weapons effective on everything except MBTs. One requirement for all AFVs is enough off-road speed to keep up with the Challenger 2s, M1A2 Abrams, and T-72 or T-80 tanks that they accompany into battle. The AFV's basic mission is to carry small infantry teams (squad-size and below) close to the fight under armor protection, then to turn them loose against enemy anti-tank missile teams hiding in the woodwork. Their secondary mission is to clean up the battlefield of those secondary threats left over after the assault of the heavy armor. These threats include enemy AFVs, personnel carriers, trucks, recovery vehicles, bunkers, logistics sites, infantry in the open, artillery batteries, and anything else that had less than an inch (2.5cm) of armor.

A FAMILY OF WARRIORS

Warriors are available as Section ("Squad" to Americans), Infantry

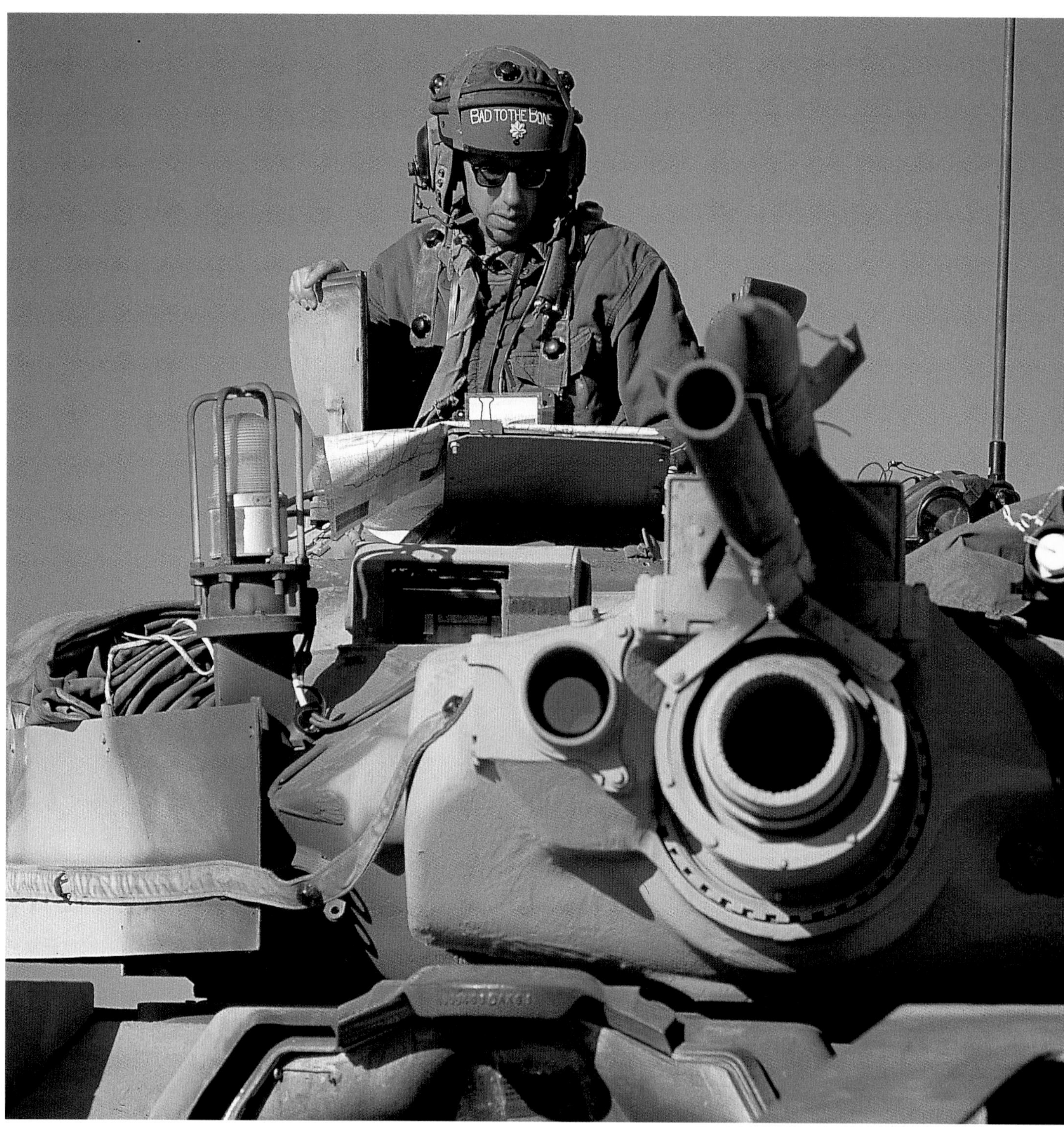

Command, Repair, Recovery, Observation Post, Artillery Command, Ambulance, and Anti-Tank Guided Missile Vehicles. All are built around a foundation that is 20 feet 6 inches (6.2m) long, 9 feet 2 inches (2.7m) high, and 9 feet 11 inches (3m) wide. The hull is welded aluminum-alloy armor, safe against ½-inch (1.2cm)/.50cal rounds, 6-inch (15.2cm) air bursts, and 20-pound (9kg) land mines. The Warrior accommodates ten soldiers, three crew, plus seven infantry. It can also carry all their kit and supplies for two days of battle.

The Warrior's power is supplied by a Perkins Rolls-Royce V-8 Condor engine. This big diesel generates 550 hp at 2300 rpm. That works out to 23 hp per ton (908kg). It can move the vehicle from 0 to 30 mph (48.2kph) in sixteen seconds, and down the road at 47 mph (75.6kph). Fuel capacity was

MAJOR WILL FOWLER (BRITISH ARMY, RETIRED) ON THE WARRIOR

People who had the Warrior in the Gulf can't say enough good things about the vehicle. One friend of mine, a company commander with the Staffords, thinks they are marvelous. With that RARDEN cannon, you can take on quite a few targets.

RARDEN was designed for use against WarPac vehicles of the BMP type, and also to take on helicopters. It is a very accurate gun, and very effective in the Gulf. My friend in the Staffords was using it against tanks, firing HESH rounds as the standard load. The HESH round was the most versatile available. It is effective against bunkers, soft-skinned vehicles, and similar targets. We all heard about an Iraqi bus engaged by American M1A1 Abrams that was firing sabot rounds. The bus took three hits without any noticeable effect. And then the bus drove off! That bus driver was the luckiest man in Iraq. If he'd been hit with HESH or HE, the bus would have been enveloped in fire.

Another virtue of RARDEN and HESH was that you could see when you got a hit. There's a visible flash. With sabot, the gunner sometimes can't evaluate the shot and wouldn't know if he had gotten a hit.

LEFT: Lt. Col. "Bad to the Bone" Monza commands the famed and feared 32nd Guards Motorized Rifle Regiment from this modified M551 Sheridan–which is supposed to look like a BMP, but doesn't–at the U.S. Army's National Training Center in the Mojave Desert.

175 gallons (662.3L), enough for up to 375 miles (603.3km) of road march.

One variant, ordered by the British Army during Desert Sabre, is the Desert Warrior. Along with the 25mm stabilized cannon and TOW missiles, the Desert Warrior provides crews with protection from the incredible heat and humidity of the Persian Gulf–it has air conditioning!

More than three hundred Warriors fought in the Gulf War, and some fought very hard indeed. The Staffords used their Warriors against everything in their way, including Iraqi MBTs, quite successfully. While the RARDEN cannon wasn't designed to defeat T-55 turret frontal armor, the impact of HESH rounds was apparently so loud and impressive that the enemy crews bailed out almost immediately after the first hit.

Warriors have been patrolling Bosnia under United Nations colors for several years, another difficult environment.

The latest addition to the family is the Warrior Reconnaissance vehicle, a basic Warrior with a TOW missile system added. It also has advanced thermal imaging sights and a suite of surveillance systems: daylight camera, IR camera, laser range finder, and battlefield surveillance radar.

LEFT: A specially configured variant, the Desert Warrior, frolics in the vast middle eastern sandbox. That 30mm cannon will handle just about any target except a main battle tank. **OPPOSITE:** This curious vehicle is a Kettenkraftrad, a motorcycle and tractor combined. It was originally designed to tow a small anti-tank gun or trailer. This one was restored by Greg Taylor. **BELOW:** Quite a few Kettenkraftrads survived the war. Many were used by forest rangers and loggers, and others by farmers–a few of whom plowed with the little machine.

Computer equipment processes, integrates, and provides secure transmission of data to the crew's parent unit. The Warrior Recon vehicle is designed for a seventy-two-hour rather than a forty-eight-hour battlefield day.

THE KLEINE KETTENKRAFTRAD NSU HK 101

One of the most interesting vehicles of World War II was the German half-track motorcycle–properly called Kleine Kettenkraftrad HK 101 ("small-tracked motorbike HK 101"), more commonly known as the Kettenkrad. The first were built in 1940 by the company of NSU Werke AG, Neckarsulm, a well-known motorcycle factory. It was promoted to the *Wehrmacht* as a good cross-country vehicle with a crew of three soldiers, and pulled either a small trailer or an anti-tank gun.

The Kettenkrad came equipped with a small one-axle trailer, with a payload capacity of 880 pounds (400kg). The trailer's wheels were identical to the front wheel of the Kettenkrad.

The first Kettenkrads saw service in Africa with Rommel's Afrika Korps. The *Wehrmacht*, however, wasn't very interested in the odd-looking little half-track. Their preference was the BMW R 75 or Zündapp KS 750 motorcycle with a sidecar. Motorcycles performed well enough during the invasion of Poland in 1939 and France in 1940. Motorcycles were simple machines, and the Kleine Kettenkraftrad HK 101 was quite complicated.

The *Wehrmacht* changed its mind, though, after Operation Barbarossa began and the German Army spent a few months in Russia. The autumn rains and spring thaw

turned roads into quagmire, impassable to most wheeled vehicles. Travel was sometimes impossible. In 1940, before Barbarossa, NSU built just 150 Kettenkrads. The next year, the *Wehrmacht* ordered many more Kettenkrads, and NSU started producing them by the thousands. The bulk of production came during 1943 (about twenty-five hundred) and 1944 (about thirty-five hundred). Toward the end of 1944, the assembly line for the Kettenkrads in the NSU factory was destroyed by Allied strategic bombing raids, and production slowed almost to a halt.

The Kettenkrad is about the size of a very large motorcycle with a sidecar. It measures about 10 feet (3m) long, 3 feet (9.4cm) wide, and weighs about 2,720 pounds (1,234.8kg). Maximum payload, including driver, is only 715 pounds (324.6kg), plus 880 pounds (400kg) for the trailer. That payload could come in the form of a couple of troops with their combat equipment, a trailer full of ammunition and supplies, or a towed small antitank cannon with its ammunition. Seats for two passenger soldiers, facing aft, and racks for their rifles were standard equipment.

The half-track is powered by a 1.5-liter OPEL 4-cylinder in-line engine. This engine was first built for the OPEL Olympia car and produced 36 hp, which was delivered to the tracks through a specialized drive-train built under license from the American Cletrac Company of Cleveland, Ohio. This gearbox offers six forward and two reverse gears. The driver steers the Kettenkrad with a handlebar. Small movements of the handlebar turn only the front fork, while larger movements actuate the steering brakes. When required, differential track speeds can be used to make tight turns.

After the war, the half-track went back into production, but only with the consent of the Allied occupying administration. Strictly speaking, military vehicles could not be produced, but NSU demonstrated that the Kettenkrad had been originally designed for civilian forestry operations. On that basis, manufacture began again. About 550 more were made from 1945 to 1948. Some were used in the U.S. and Canada by timber businesses and the U.S. Forest Service. Other Kettenkrads were sold as tractors, but the design's complex drivetrain and relatively small drawbar power made them impractical on the farm.

An estimated total of about eight thousand Kettenkrads were built, but production figures vary somewhat. Most of those built for the war went to the eastern front.

After the war, in the late 1950s, Germany built a new army, the Bundeswehr. NSU developed a modern version of the Kettenkrad, called Gebirgskarette, and offered it to the Bundeswehr. The Bundeswehr refused the offer.

Quite a few vintage Kettenkrads are still around and running. They show up regularly at demonstrations and in military vehicle collections.

THE GROßE KETTENKRAFTRAD NSU HK 102

The HK 101 was the Kleine Kettenkrad. There were also proto-

SPECIFICATIONS	Kleines Kettenkraftrad
Full name	Kleines Kettenkraftrad HK 101 or Kleines Kettenkrad HK 101 ("Krad" is the military short form of "Kraftrad," which means "motorbike")
Crew	3
Manufacturer	NSU Werke AG, Neckarsulm
Type	HK 101
***Wehrmacht* type**	SdKfz 2 (Special vehicle No. 2)
Weight	2,720 lbs (1.2t)
Permament total weight	3,435 lbs (1.6t)
Length	10 ft (3m)
Height	3 ft 5 in (1m)
Width	3 ft (91.4cm)
Payload	715 lbs (324.6kg) (including driver) on the vehicle, 880 lbs (400kg) on the trailer
Top speed	44 mph (70.7kph)
Engine	OPEL (GM) 1.5-liter 4-cylinder in-line overhead valve, output 36 hp
Steering	Wide bends only with the front wheel. Sharp bends actuate the steering brakes of the tracks. Steering gear made under license of the Cleveland Tractor Company (Cletrac).
Gearbox	Six forward, two reverse gears
Tracks	Lubricated tracks with two needle bearings and two shaft sealing rings in each track link. Each link has a grease chamber, containing 7 oz (200g) grease. (One track has forty links.)
Years of production	1940–1948. After WWII, from 1945–1948, around 550 Kettenkrads were built as tractors with the permission of the Allies.

MY KETTENKRAD

I bought my Kettenkrad in 1992 in the former East Germany. It was used by a farmer as a farm tractor. The farmer had thrown away all the parts of the superstructure that he didn't need (toolbox, battery box, one of the two fuel tanks, hood, rear seats). Then he had welded some hard points to the hull to fit a plow. There was a different engine (1.2-liter SV OPEL engine instead of the 1.5-liter OHV OPEL engine). The original driver's seat was gone. The farmer used a kitchen chair to sit on! There was a different front fork and front wheel (from a BMW R75 WW2 motorbike) and there were no working brakes. The farmer used the brake of the motorbike front wheel to stop the 1.5 tons (1.3t) of the Kettenkrad.

My Kettenkrad has the chassis number 111533. So it is number 1533 of all. (The leading "11" says that it is a Kettenkrad HK 101.) It must have been built in late 1942 or early 1943. I don't know the exact production date, because the data plate is missing. NSU says that they don't have the production records anymore.

It took a lot of work to get the missing parts and to bring the vehicle back to its original condition. The hull and the superstructure are (nearly) complete now, but it was a lot of work to bring the Kettenkrad on the road. Registration for use on public roads is not a big problem in Germany.

It's a pity that I don't know more about the history of my Kettenkrad, but it is hard to get information about Wehrmacht *vehicles in Germany. Many records were destroyed at the end of the war and most of the rest were taken by the Allies.*

ANDREAS MEHLHORN, Braunschweig, Germany

BELOW: Steering the Kettenkrad is a bit of a challenge; normal front-wheel control works fine for slow turns, but the driver must use track braking for tighter maneuvering.

types of a bigger version, called Großes Kettenkrad ("big-tracked motorbike"), type HK 102. The HK 102 was 6 inches (15.2cm) wider and 12 inches (30.4cm) longer, and was able to carry six soldiers (including the driver). The HK 102 had a Ford V-8 engine instead of the OPEL 4-in-line of the small HK 101. The 102 also had one more wheel on each side. Only prototypes were built of the 102. Though there are some (very rare) photographs of the HK 102, no vehicles survived.

FERRET AND FOX

One of history's most successful military vehicles is the British armored recon vehicle known as the Ferret. The foundation of Ferret design goes back to before World War II with the Daimler Dingo scout car. Other than the name–and some improvements in the engine and other systems–the Ferret hasn't really changed very much since. While the name might have been changed a few times, the essence has remained the same. Only in the late 1990s was the design

OODD95

LEFT: Certainly one of the least sophisticated and most successful light armored vehicles of all time, the little British Ferret puttered around the world, keeping a lid on many simmering hot spots. This one is in use by two officers keeping the peace on Cyprus in the 1970s.

finally retired from the active British Army. Recently, many were sold to overseas clients and to collectors.

The Ferret's biography begins right after World War II, when a replacement for the Dingo scout car was needed. The new scout car had to be fast, wheeled, and light, and have sufficient armor to protect the two-man crew from small-arms fire and artillery splinters. Only hits from directly overhead would go unprotected, as the commander's cupola was open to the sky.

The contract was awarded in 1948, the first prototype was delivered in 1949, and, after the usual test and evaluation phase, the design was accepted in 1950 and designated Car Scout 4X4 Liaison (Ferret Mk 1) FV701C.

Even before the first production Mk 1 rolled out Daimler's door, the British Army contracted with the company for another variant, the Mk 2, with a turret and .30cal Browning machine gun. The second version is slightly taller, holds a three-man crew, and adds overhead protection. Daimler delivered the first production models of both the Mk 1 and Mk 2 in 1952, and would continue to manufacture them for twenty years. The last of 4,409 was delivered in 1971.

FERRET DESCRIPTION

The Ferret is a four-wheel-drive, rear-engine, gasoline-drinking vehicle. It is built upon a sheet-steel hull. Mk 1 versions are armed with just a single .30cal Browning M1919A4 or Bren LMG 7.62mm machine gun, mounted outside the cupola. Both of these weapons require the commander to expose himself to hostile fire during engagements.

Armor on the Ferret varies from about ½ inch (1.2cm) on the front of the hull to about ¼ inch (6mm) on most of the hull floor. The whole package, full of gas, guns, crew, and ammunition, weighs in at about 4½ tons (4t).

All Ferrets are powered by a Rolls-Royce B60 Mk 6A engine, with output ranging from 116 hp for the Mk 1 to 129 hp for the Mk 4. This engine is completely waterproof and allows the Ferret to wade streams up to about 5½ feet (1.6m) with minimal preparation. The engine powers the vehicle through an innovative H-shaped drive line, with driveshafts for the left- and right-side wheels running parallel along the sides of the vehicle. This is unlike other recon types, which had the driveshaft on the centerline. The H-shaped line allows a lower driver's position, and makes for a lower vehicle overall. The transmission is a Daimler preselect 5-speed. This design helped make the Ferret as quick and agile as its namesake, and about as mobile as anything on

MAJOR WILL FOWLER (BRITISH ARMY, RETIRED) ON THE FOX AND FERRET

Ferret is an excellent little patrol vehicle, having served in the Gulf, in Northern Ireland, against insurgents in British Malaya in the late 1950s and 1960s, and was even used by the French in Algeria during their war there during the 1960s. It has always been very popular for reconnaissance duties. An engineer company commander can use one to dash up to a possible site for a river crossing, take a look around, then get away quickly. It has the armor protection and speed you want for something like that. Also, it has been used extensively in Northern Ireland where tracked vehicles have been considered too "military" and "provocative" and are not used at all.

Both Fox and Ferret have had a tipping problem, more so with Fox. The temptation with both vehicles is to drive them fast, and the commander typically is standing "proud" of the hatch, with his head and shoulders sticking out. When the thing gets rolling and then tips, the commander is likely to end up badly.

The Ferret has been used operationally around the globe by British forces, and is a much-loved vehicle, despite the problems with rolling. It is fast, reliable, and good enough to replace its own replacement, the Fox.

the battlefield. Its road speed is 55 mph (88.4kph), and it has a range of 180 miles (289.6km).

All Ferrets are a bit top-heavy. The Mk 2, with its added turret, has an especially high center of gravity and occasionally tips over on sharp, fast turns.

Mk 2's turret is powered only by the commander's muscles. It lacks any sophisticated vision systems, although it does mount an AFV No. 3 Mk 1 periscope. The gun elevates to +45 degrees and can depress to −15. With twenty-five hundred rounds stowed in the hull, the Ferret can create a lot of mischief.

After fifteen years of honorable service to the Crown, the Ferret seemed to be getting a little weary for the modern battlefield. Thus in 1966 the British Army asked for bids on a new version. This new light recon vehicle was yet another pumped-up Daimler Dingo, this time with a hard-

hitting 30mm RARDEN cannon and aluminum armor. It is called the Fox, and it entered British service in 1970.

FOX DESCRIPTION

Powered by a big 195-hp Jaguar 6-cylinder engine, the Fox is rated to 60 mph (96.5kph). The Fox's turret is much larger than the Ferret's, but it is still cramped. There is no turret basket, but there is a little footrest to help keep feet from getting tangled in the works. There is no place at all for a tall gunner's knees; the elevation control is squarely in the way.

The sights are big and bright, however, with a good night sight just below the optical day version. The Fox is generously equipped with vision blocks, too. The gunner and commander have good vision across the turret front, but can't see to the rear without traversing the turret.

OPPOSITE: This Ferret's urban camouflage scheme is unique to the British Berlin Brigade, back in the dark days of the cold war. ABOVE: Another view of the Ferret. This one is owned by a military vehicle collector, Carl Barredo.

SPECIFICATIONS	Ferret Mk 2
Crew	2
Weight	9,700 lbs (4,403.8kg)
Length with gun forward	12 ft 10 in (3.9m)
Turret height	5 ft 6 in (1.6m)
Width	6 ft 3 in (1.9m)
Ground clearance	13 in (33cm)
Propulsion	Rolls-Royce B60 Mk 6A 6-cylinder gasoline engine producing 129 hp
Transmission	Daimler preselect 5-speed
Speed	58 mph (93kph) max (road)
Acceleration	0 to 30 mph (48.2km) in 3.6 seconds
Range	188 miles (306km)
Obstacle crossing	Vertical: 16 in (40.6cm) Trench: 46 in (1.1m) with channels
Main armament	7.62mm machine gun

ABOVE: Another offspring of the British Ferret, this sturdy six-wheeled FV 601 Saladin offers more protection, mobility, and firepower, plus a little more room for the crew.

The Fox driver has, in many ways, the best seat in the house. His compartment is comparatively spacious, with good instrumentation on the right side, and a steering wheel mounted up and down, like a ship's wheel. On some Foxes the driver also serves as the chief cook, since a small electrical oven is mounted on the bulkhead by his right shoulder–just the thing for making a good cup of tea.

INDIAN MOTORCYCLE (USA WWII)

Motorcycles have been zipping around the edges of the battlefield for about eighty years now, since World War I, when many were used for courier work. You'll still find them assigned to many U.S. and British units, particularly to recon units and scouts. They still dash around today in the scorching desert at the National Training Center, in California, sneaking and peeking at the enemy forces and reporting back to the Tactical Operations Center (TOC).

A tremendous variety of motorcycles were used during World War II by all the European nations. One example of the breed is the Indian 340B, a military vehicle much in demand by collectors.

The 340B was more commonly called the Military Chief, a customized version of Indian's successful civilian Chief line of motorcycles from the 1930s. Indian started producing the Military Chief in large numbers during 1940, including one large order for the French Army. About half of this order for five thousand machines were lost when the freighter carrying them across the Atlantic, the SS *Hanseatic Star*, was torpedoed by the Germans and sunk.

The Indian Military Chiefs used a tried-and-true 1200cc V-twin engine and 3-speed transmission, all tucked into a sturdy tubular steel frame. The front fork and rear wheel suspension are both built tough in anticipation of rough service.

The advent of the jeep, and its tremendous popularity with the troops as well as the public, reduced the need for motorcycles in the U.S. Army. As a result, many military contracts for motorcycles were canceled in the early 1940s. Large numbers of completed military machines were sold by Indian to the public, most of which were converted to civilian colors. A few, though, were unmodified, and these rare specimens are extremely valuable today.

JEEP

The little jeep, without doubt, has become the most popular American military vehicle of World War II. Thousands survived to be collected, restored, used for backwoods travel, and shown off in parades. Americans and their WWII Allies fell in love with the little ¼-ton (227kg) vehicle back in the early 1940s, and the love affair hasn't died yet. You'll find them all over the world—in England, Scotland, Norway, France, Australia, Canada, and, of course, the United States.

The jeep was born in 1940 with a U.S. Army development program for combat vehicles. It was obvious by that time that America couldn't avoid involvement in the growing European conflict. It was also obvious that the army—which had just surrendered its trusty horses, under protest, in favor of trucks and flimsy little tanks—would need to go to war on wheels and tracks instead of hooves. At the same time as heavy and medium trucks were being designed and tested for this new vision of a "mechanized" army, the Army added a requirement for a small liaison and personnel transport vehicle.

Although they called it a truck, the resulting design was what we call today a sport utility vehicle, with many of the same features. It was intended to carry up to four soldiers. The army came up with a set of basic specifications, then contracted with three vendors for prototype vehicles.

One of the three prototypes, the BRC, came from the now-forgotten Bantam Car Company of Butler, Pennsylvania. The first samples of BRCs arrived in 1941—a total of 2,642 were built that year, some of them with four-wheel steering. Another version, designated the GP (General Purpose), came from the Ford Motor Company of

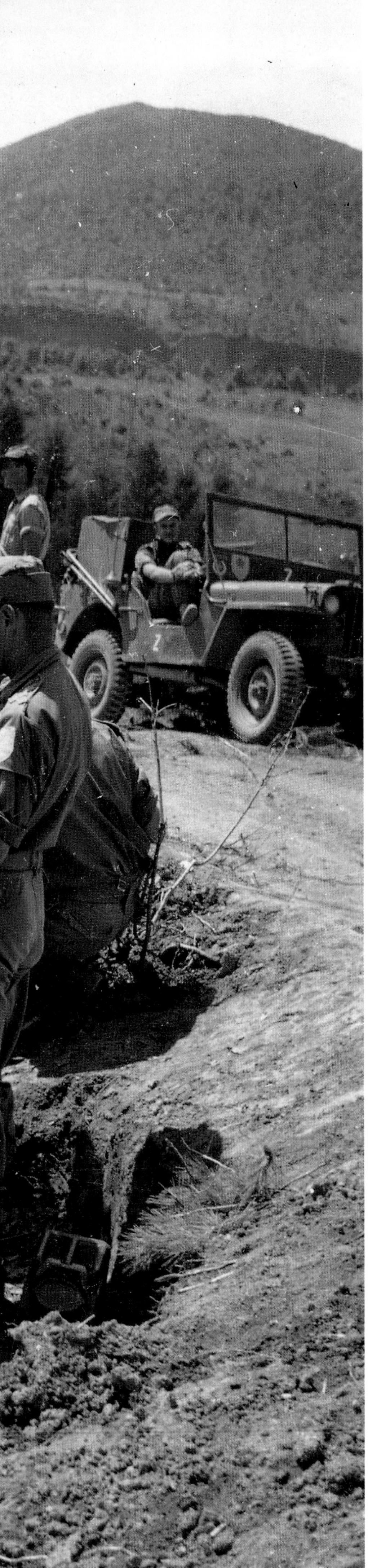

LEFT: A small fleet of jeeps escorts an M8 Armored Car, all from the Canadian Army's Lord Strathcona's Horse regiment. The unit is covering an infantry advance in Korea.

Dearborn, Michigan. Some thirty-seven hundred Ford GPs were also delivered in 1941.

The third version came from the Willys company. These were initially designated the MA. Willys won the contract, and the MA was accepted as the standard ¼-ton (227kg) truck for the new action army, 1941 style. The army's demand for vehicles was so large that Willys couldn't begin to fill it, so some of the production was shifted to Ford under license.

NAME THAT VEHICLE!

Nobody knows exactly where the name "jeep" came from, but several versions of the story are part of the jeep's legend and lore. One story claims the name came from a character in an April 1936 Popeye cartoon strip, an odd little animal named Eugene the jeep. Another tale says the name's origin came from an oil exploration company that called a little all-terrain vehicle used for exploration "jeep." The U.S. Army was also referring to its experimental autogyro as "jeep" around then. Some say Irvin "Red" Hausmann, a test driver for Willys during 1940, first attached the name to the little 4X4. Finally, and most likely, it is said that the name evolved from the Ford GP. The "GP" started being pronounced as "jeep," and the moniker stuck.

Early on, however, the name was hardly universal. For a year or so, the Army insisted on calling the little vehicle a "peep," based on its intended recon role. Imaginative caption writers at popular magazines insisted on calling it the Blitz Bunny, Puddle-Jumper, and Bug. *The Washington Post's* Katherine Hillyer popularized the term "jeep" in an article about the vehicle printed on February 19, 1941, in which she wrote that Red Hausmann was asked by someone what his little vehicle was called. "It's a 'jeep,'" he said.

And so it was–from then on.

There was still dissent. The Army, and particularly Colonel Charles Black (who was in charge of the test-and-development program at Fort Knox, Kentucky) really wanted to use "jeep" for a larger vehicle, and "peep" for the little ¼-ton (227kg) Command and Reconnaissance Truck. The army persisted in the name confusion until Colonel Black surrendered to popular sentiment in December 1943.

JEEP DESCRIPTION

Jeeps started rolling off the assembly line at a tremendous rate. They were an immediate hit with the American public. They were a hit with the British, Russian, and Canadian public, too, because it was to these countries that many of the first ones went, sent to aid U.S. Allies. By the time production was all over, four years later, Willys had built 350,349 of the MB

ABOVE & OPPOSITE: Many thousands of jeeps were sold after World War II in Europe and North America. Here's one of the survivors on display in England, restored to the way it might have appeared in service to the legendary 101st Airborne Division fifty years ago.

version and Ford had delivered 281,578 very slightly different GPWs.

Each of them weighs 2,450 pounds (1,112.3kg) empty and 3,650 pounds (1,657.1kg) fully loaded. The jeep is an amazingly simple vehicle, which probably has a lot to do with its success. The engine is a small (134 cubic inches), economical 4-cylinder water-cooled in-line L-head, with a cast-iron block and head, only three crank bearings, mechanical valve lifters, and a low compression ratio of about 6.5 to 1. Wound up to a screaming 4000 rpm, the engine delivers 54 hp. Range is 285 miles (458.5km). Top speed is 65 mph (104.5kph), a welcome swiftness when fleeing a force of Panzers and infantry.

The chassis is amazingly compact. The wheelbase measures 80 inches (2m), the overall length is 132 inches (3.3m), and it is 62 inches (1.5m) wide. With the windshield and canvas top up, the jeep measures 6 feet (1.8m) high, but both fold down to make for a much more compact vehicle.

The transmission is planted firmly in the center of the vehicle. It has three speeds forward, one reverse, with a two-speed transfer case, driving four 6.00X16.6 military nondirectional tires. Some jeeps use 6-volt electrical systems, while those equipped with radios have 12 volts.

Jeeps served everywhere, went everywhere, did everything. Some had machine guns mounted on a pintle between the front seats. Jeeps prowled the back roads of France, the Low Countries, Italy, and Germany, sometimes ahead of the heavy armor, looking for suitable routes for the advance. They carried senior—and junior—officers, as well as NCOs. They went back to the field kitchens to bring hot chow forward to the troops in the line. They brought up ammunition, mail, and water. Rigged with racks for litters, jeeps carried dead and wounded soldiers back to aid stations and field hospitals—and brought back fresh, green replacements.

The jeep had only one bad habit: it rolled over. Many soldiers died in them during World War II when the driver attempted a corner at too high a

Property of the 101st A/B
XSK 114
101 AB
PXI

SOME JEEP FACTS FROM ANDY CARTER (JEEPMAN@COMPUSERVE.COM)

• In the early 1940s, U.S. Army officials used "peep" as the preferred name to classify the ¼-ton (227kg) 4X4 Command and Reconnaissance Truck and described larger half-ton (454kg) vehicles as the true army jeep. Unfortunately neither soldiers nor the general public saw it that way. The use of the name as a generic term for ¼-ton (227kg) vehicles was not officially recognized until Colonel Claude A. Black at Fort Knox formally accepted defeat on the matter in December 1943.

• The 1942 Willys maintenance manual issued with each vehicle contained a wealth of information relating to routine maintenance and repair. It also contained tips for emergency repairs that included how to deal with bullet holes in the radiator. (Now there's a bit of information you won't find in a modern-day Haynes manual.) Punctures are a nuisance at any time—but all the more so on a WWII battlefield with bullets and shrapnel flying. Fortunately, the risk could be reduced by fitting bullet-resisting inner tubes, which were made of thicker and heavier materials than the standard type, with the result that bullet punctures were automatically sealed. Their green painted valve stems could generally identify these tubes.

• WWII jeep trailers were designed to float—useful if you have to get them across a deep river—but how to get the jeep across? Well, it could be done by standing the jeep on a large canvas sheet, which was then pulled up around it to make it into a sort of boat. I have seen a picture of this but don't intend to try it with mine.

• Mr. Shafer, president of the Horseless Carriage Club of Los Angeles, was one of the first civilians to own a jeep before the war had completely ended. A photograph of him proudly standing beside the vehicle on June 25, 1944, appeared on the front cover of the club's magazine in September of that same year.

• One could be forgiven for mistakenly thinking that more jeeps must have been produced for use during World War II than any other military vehicle. However, this is not the case. In reality more GMC trucks (Jimmies) were manufactured in their various forms during 1939–45.

• The MB jeep was used as the basis for the first prototype Land Rover built after the war for Maurice Wilks, a director of the Rover Company. The prototype Land Rover combined many jeep parts. These included the chassis, suspension, and transmission—combined with a Rover engine, gearbox, and steering. He was so pleased with the resulting vehicle that the company went on to design and produce the Series 1 Land Rover in 1948.

• When it was launched in July 1950, the civilian CJ3 version of the M38 jeep was priced at $1,090. Prices have risen somewhat over the years, and not just for good examples of the full-size vehicle. Both sizes appeared diminutive—like Dinky toys manufactured by Meccano—during the 1950s. WWII jeeps, of course, saw all sorts of modifications for civilian use after the war.

• The most unusual U.K. jeep was the one customized to carry shooting parties about on the Bowes-Lyons (Queen Mother's family) estate in County Durham. A local blacksmith subsequently used it as a mobile welding truck and its condition deteriorated. It finally ended up in a scrap yard for spares in 1970.

• The thought of seeing a six-wheel conversion to an MB/GPW at a custom car show must be every military enthusiast's worst nightmare. Amazingly, such a 6X6 beast was actually produced during World War II by Ford. However, it was found during the 1941 trials that it had no real advantages over the ¾-ton (681kg) Dodge Weapons Carrier. It never went into production.

• French Army jeeps often had groups of twelve notches cut or filed into the steering wheel. The notches did not form part of any approved military modification but were added by conscripts recording the passing of their twelve-month national service.

BELOW: An M151 toward the end of its service life, soon to be replaced by the Hummer.

speed, or when a wheel went into a ditch. The vehicle provided no protection at all in rollovers, and if the canvas top was erected–preventing passengers from being ejected from a wreck–the result was typically fatal for one or all hands.

After the war most jeeps were left overseas and used for landfill, along with perfectly good aircraft, tanks, and other equipment. Some jeeps were sold for civilian use, where they were converted to tractors or utility vehicles. In the Philippines, many were converted to taxis. Back in the U.S., many thousands were bought by ex-servicemen and used for backcountry travel on hunting and fishing trips.

Jeeps are probably the most popular and sought-after military vehicles today. WWII models fetch up to $15,000, depending on condition. M38s and M151s from the 1950s and 1960s are worth up to $10,000 in mint and complete condition. They are extremely popular among collectors in England, Scotland, Norway, and even Finland, where jeeps served the Finnish Army and were then sold off to the public.

JEEPS IN ACTION

Jeeps saw plenty of action and thousands of bullet wounds during World War II–and even subsequently. Captain David Sterling's famous Special Air Service (SAS), a special operations unit developed during the war by the British Army, started using Jeeps in 1941 for rapid strike missions against the Italians and Germans in North Africa. The first raid, in December 1941, attacked two airfields. Sixty-one aircraft went up in flames. Soon after, another raid destroyed twenty-seven more planes. A few months later, the SAS raiders had fifteen jeeps in action.

All the jeeps were heavily modified. Windshields and all unessential parts were stripped. Twin Vickers K .303cal machine guns were installed in a flexible anti-aircraft mount. An ingenious condenser was mounted in front of the radiator to collect coolant overflow. Some jeeps mounted five machine guns, firing a mix of tracer, ball, and AP rounds. This was an extremely effective combination when used against airplanes and unarmored vehicles. Later, for operation in Europe, armor plate was added.

The basic SAS tactic involved night marches across terrain considered impassable and undefended, then a rapid strike across a remote airfield, guns blazing. The jeep's ability to zoom around at faster than 50 mph (80.4kph) made it tough to hit.

After D-day, SAS raiders dropped jeeps and 144 raiders near the city of Dijon. Near the town of Les Ormes, two jeeps and four SAS raiders attacked two Nazi staff vehicles and a truck full of soldiers. The attack killed or wounded more than sixty German SS.

END OF THE LINE–M151

While not officially a jeep, the paternity of the M151 is obvious. It is a little ¼-ton (227kg) truck with exactly the same mission in life as the old MB or GPW. Although the design details are different–with independent 4-wheel

6 7

OPPOSITE & BELOW: Kerry Johnson's M151A1 is a 1967 product of the Ford Motor Company. The M60 machine gun is a nonfiring replica, one of the many accessories available to collectors. Even without it mounted, Johnson is occasionally stopped by highway patrol officers wondering why a civilian is driving a military vehicle on the street.

suspension, a 4-speed instead of 3-speed transmission, and some cosmetic changes—the M151A1 still provides uncomfortable, breezy seating for four. The new jeep still goes just about anywhere and despite the makover, it still rolls over at the first opportunity.

Today, that propensity of those first M151s to roll—when driven too fast by an inexperienced or poorly trained driver—has made the M151 a rare and debated model within the collector movement. You'll see a few M151s running around at some shows, although the U.S. government claims no such vehicles were ever sold to private individuals. Regardless, many are somehow available for sale.

Some apparently were sold through the Defense Reutilization and Marketing Office (DRMO). Others were assembled from individually purchased parts. The Army has claimed the M151 wasn't a safe vehicle to sell to the public, and threatened to reclaim privately owned vehicles.

One Military Vehicle Preservation Association (MVPA) official says,

"Even if you properly bought a M151 from the U.S. government, and have all the paperwork to back you up, there is still the possibility that a government agent can show up someday and say, 'You don't have the right to have that vehicle, and I am going to confiscate it!'" An M151A2 was advertised for sale in California in 1998 for $4,500.

M151s were built from 1960 to 1969 by both AM General and Ford Motor Company. They served until the 1980s, when they were replaced by the Hummer.

LAND ROVER—THE JEEP LEGACY

In many ways, the real legacy of the old Willys jeep lives on in the British Land Rover, a vehicle whose design

evolved directly from that little ¼-ton (227kg) truck. Like the Frankenstein monster, the first Land Rover (Land Rover 1) was assembled, in 1948, from the parts of dead jeeps. It quickly became a worldwide success of its own. Land Rovers today are used by many armies, in many roles.

ABOVE: **Jack Valenti's Long Range Desert Group truck re-creates a vehicle that saw extensive British service in North Africa. This one is complete with maps, rifles, and water-cooled Browning machine gun appropriate to its old mission.** **LEFT:** **This Land Rover is on safari and looking for big game–the kind that shoots back. That's a Mk 19 grenade launcher on top, a 7.62mm machine gun below.**

THE DEFENDER SERIES

The current family of Land Rover military vehicles are called Defenders, and members of the family come in several sizes. The smallest, the Defender 90, is a jeep-type vehicle designed for extreme off-road conditions. It has accommodations for a crew of three to seven people. Four engines are available, including a nonturbo-charged diesel and three gasoline models. In British service, the Defender 90 is designated the Truck, Utility, Light (TUL), and serves in many capacities. One of these is as a light ambulance–a simple utility model. Another is as a gun jeep that mounts twin 7.62mm machine guns, a MILAN missile launcher, or a 106mm recoilless rifle.

DEFENDER 110

British forces call the basic Defender 110 a TUM (no smart remarks, please) for Truck, Utility, Medium, and use it extensively for both general cargo and radio truck applications, designated the GSC and FFR variants, respectively. The TUM is large for a jeep-type vehicle and can absorb 1½ tons (1.3t) of payload. A typical payload is three hefty British lads in full kit, plus up to ten more of their mates in back.

The Defender 110 gets its go-power from one of several engines: a 2.5-liter turbo-charged diesel generating 107 hp; a 3.5-liter V-8 gasoline version generating 134 hp; or a 2.5-liter in-line 4-cylinder gasoline engine.

RIGHT: Well, it seemed like a good idea at the time...but this huge 30mm cannon seems like overkill, even on the sturdy Land Rover Multi Role Combat Vehicle 90-series chassis.

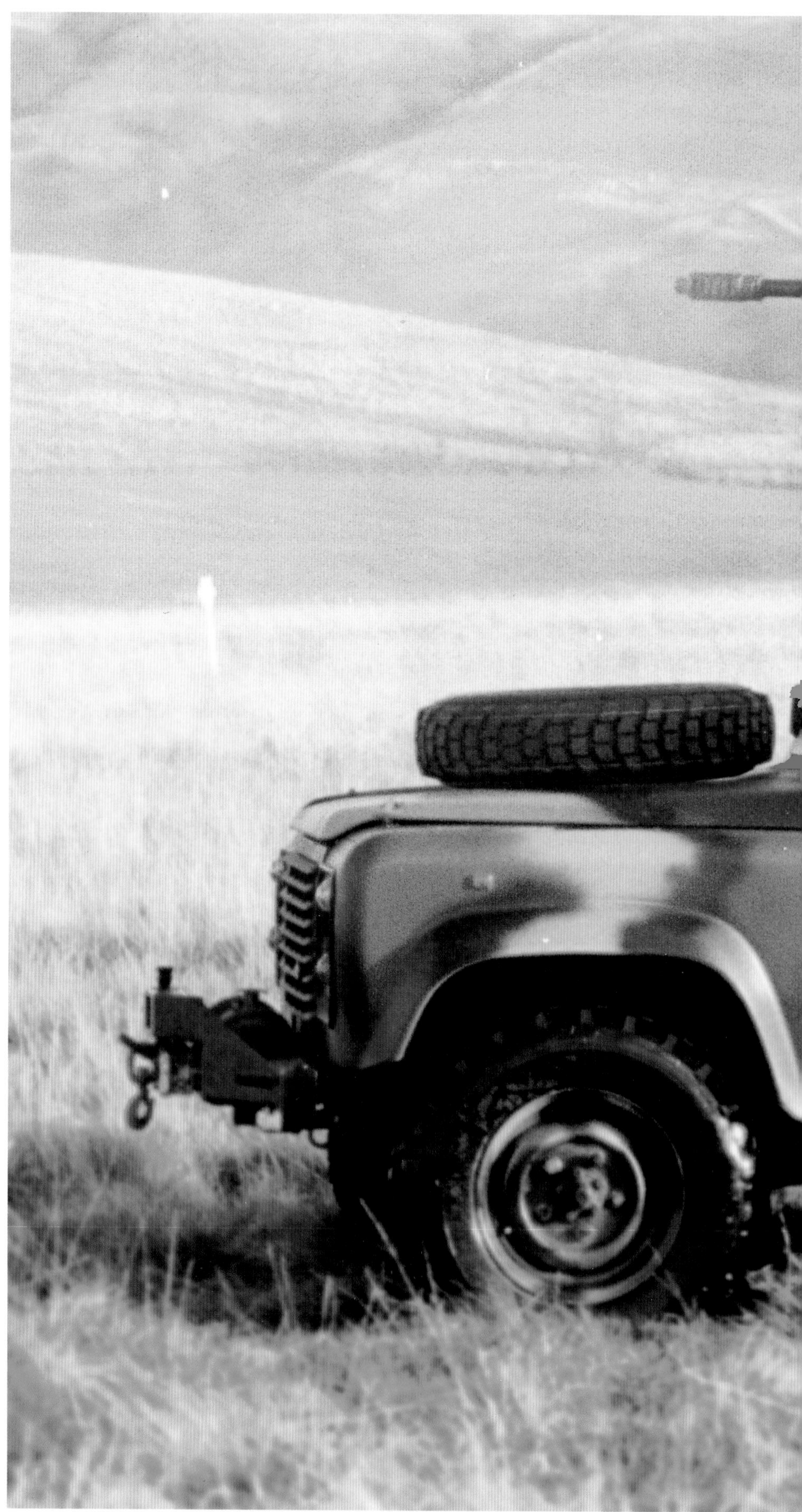

That last power plant produces 83 hp. It is linked to a 5-speed manual transmission that powered all four wheels through a two-speed transfer case.

Thousands of these vehicles are still in service with Commonwealth nations, including twenty-five hundred built in Australia for that nation's army. Examples still serve with the armies of Turkey, Ireland, and other countries.

DEFENDER 110 MULTI ROLE COMBAT VEHICLE (MRCV)

The most interesting version of the Defender 110 is the Multi Role Combat Vehicle (MRCV). It is a gun jeep on steroids. The original Defender MRCV is a revised Land Rover with coil springs and a modified body, aimed in the early 1980s at the commercial market. The first military sale came a year later. It soon turned into a very popular item among armed forces worldwide. It had no armor at all and was reliant on speed, agility, and its compact size to evade enemy notice.

Ah, but the MRCV can pack a punch. Rigged with a Mark 19 40mm grenade launcher, it can beat up troops, in the open or under cover, and defeat thin-skinned vehicles anywhere inside around 760 yards (694.9m). When it is time to skedaddle, the MRCV evaporates into the woodwork.

CHAPTER SEVENTEEN

COMBAT SUPPORT

M88 RECOVERY VEHICLE

No armor unit ever wants to be far away from a big, well-equipped recovery vehicle, and one of the biggest and best is the huge M88. The M88 makes even the big M1 Abrams look small and insignificant.

The M88's hull is fabricated from cast- and rolled-sheet armor welded together into a massive, rigid foundation. A large crane attachment lifts any tank component, including turrets, and even complete vehicles weighing up to 14,150 pounds (6.4t). A blade at the front helps stabilize the vehicle during lifting or winching operations.

Five crewmen are assigned to an M88. They get some of the grimiest, most difficult missions of any support personnel. They have to break and replace tracks in the mud, pull engines, extract bogged tanks and trucks, and tow them all back to the motor pool. Power for all of that muscle is provided by a 750-hp V-12 air-cooled diesel linked to a 4-speed automatic transmission. Even with all that horsepower, the M88 is good for only 26 mph (41.8kph) on a good road. But with a full tank (341 gallons [1,290.8L] of fuel), the M88 has range: 280 miles (450.5km).

Although the crew rarely sees combat, they know to expect the unexpected. A .50cal heavy machine gun is installed over the vehicle commander's hatch, and all the mechanics have brackets for their M16s. They are likely to use them, too, especially for exercises at NTC, where the OPFOR loves to sneak up on the complacent rear-support area units and shoot them up while they are busy fixing tanks.

HEAVY EXPANDED MOBILITY TACTICAL TRUCK (HEMTT)

Tanks may get all the glory, but they don't go anywhere without a long line of trucks following behind, keeping them and their crews in business. In fact, it takes two trucks to keep one tank in action–or it used to, until the huge HEMTT joined the Army.

HEMTT (pronounced "hemitt" by the troops) is the acronym for Heavy Expanded Mobility Tactical Truck, a very large 8-wheel-drive transporter built by Oshkosh Truck Corporation. It has been in use by the U.S. Army since the mid-1980s. You can see them roar-

RIGHT: The huge M88 Recovery Vehicle dwarfs even the big M1 Abrams main battle tank–and just about everything else that moves on land. Here's one pulling a power pack from another one in the field, a fairly quick and common chore for the M88 and its crew.

LEFT: Eating dust or mud, right behind the advancing tanks, will be found the unsung heroes of all armored units, the logistics support units with their huge HEMTT fuel tankers. These big trucks have an unusual flexible chassis that allows cross-country travel. ABOVE: Another version of the HEMTT is designed for palletized cargo–ammunition, barrier material, MREs, and anything else required by the combat units forward.

ing around the tactical training areas at NTC, Fort Carson, Colorado, Fort Hood, Texas, and anywhere else armored units prepare to fight. They bring up fuel, barrier material for the engineers, MREs (Meals Ready to Eat, the current U.S. Army field ration), and ammunition by the ton, and deliver it all to wherever tanks go.

The M978 version of the HEMTT is a huge tanker. It carries 2,138 gallons (8,092L) of fuel. The M977 is the plain vanilla version–a cargo carrier with a small crane attached to the rear of the cargo deck. It carries about 10 tons (9t) worth of anything the deployed units need in bulk. There are also wrecker and heavy cargo versions, and a new variant called the Palletized Load System (PLS) truck, for handling palletized cargo.

All are powered by a 445-hp 8-cylinder Detroit Diesel engine coupled to a 4-speed Allison automatic transmission. The eight powered wheels give the HEMTT excellent off-road mobility, although it does sometimes get stuck. A winch is mounted on the front bumper of many for self-recovery.

THE "BEEP"

SPECIFICATIONS	M37 ¾-ton (681kg) truck
Crew	1
Weight	5,687 lbs (2.5t) without winch, 5,917 lbs (2.6t) with winch
Length	15 ft 4 in (4.6m) without winch, 15 ft 9 in (4.8m) with winch
Height	7 ft 2 in (2.2m)
Width	6 ft. 1½in (1.8m)
Ground clearance	10 in (25.4cm)
Winch	Braden LU-4, 7,500 lb (3.4t) capacity, 7⁄16 in (1.1cm) by 150 ft (45.7m)
Propulsion	Dodge L-head T-245 230.2 cu in displacement, 94 hp at 3400 rpm with compression ratio of 6.7 to 1
Carburetor	Carter ETW-1 single-barrel downdraft type
Transmission	Model 420 Helical gear synchroshift; four forward, one reverse gear
Transfer case	New Process model 200 2-speed divorce mounted transfer case
Speed	70kph on road, 10kph in water
High range ratio	1 to 1
Low range ratio	1:96 to 1

During World War II, when the jeep was hot stuff and cute nicknames were being invented for all sorts of equipment, some wise guy started calling the WC ¾-ton (681kg) 4X4 a "beep," and the name stuck.

Generations of U.S. Army soldiers have driven and admired the sturdy, dependable, capable M37 truck, and now generations of military vehicle collectors are beginning the second phase of this excellent vehicle's diverse life. The M37 was a military version of the pickup truck, a vehicle you could hop in, fire up, and use to move 1,500 pounds (681kg) of cargo or people to just about any place on dry land.

The M37 was the direct descendant of several excellent WWII light off-road trucks that were developed for the U.S. Army by the U.S. Army, and then built by Dodge. It was used by many nations during and after that war. Among its first descendants was the WC series of light trucks issued in 1941, even before the United States entered the war.

Early M37 versions had a very short 84-inch (2.1m) wheelbase (the early WC series had a wheelbase of 116 inches [2.9m]), a 6-volt electrical system, and hard bench seats that looked like they had been removed from grandpa's old buggy. Dodge fixed that little problem soon enough, and the design that would stay in production for more than twenty years was born.

Most early versions of the M37—known officially at first as the WC52—have a 98-inch (2.4m) wheel-base, lower sills, simplified bodywork, a 6-volt electrical system (command cars and carryalls had 12 volts for radios), divided combat wheels, conventional seats, and brackets for a 5-gallon (18.9L) fuel can. A winch on the front of the 52 was great for dragging jeeps and other wayward vehicles out of the mud of France and Belgium, and out of the wadis of the Sahara. Nearly sixty thousand WC52s were built during World War II.

An even more popular variant is the almost identical WC51, a slightly shorter vehicle that lacks the winch. It is about 295 pounds (133.9kg) lighter, at 5,675 pounds (2.5t). This truck and all the others in the series use a Dodge T-214 6-cylinder L-head engine that displaces 230 cubic inches. Wound up to 3200 rpm, this engine can produce 92 hp. All the Dodge ¾-ton (681kg) trucks use a 4-speed manual transmission with a two-position transfer case for engaging the front-wheel drive (WC ½- and ¾-ton [454 and 681kg] trucks use a single-speed transfer case; WC-63 1½-ton [1.3t] uses 2-speed). When the sergeant isn't watching, it is possible (as the author can attest) to get these trucks up to 60 mph (96.5kph), although the whine of those big tires on the pavement can be intense.

Several versions of the WC series vehicle were built during the war, including a telephone lineman's truck and a command recon vehicle. There was also a staff car model, complete with fold-down step, softer springs, shock absorbers, and map table for the "staff pukes" and "headquarters weenies."

An improved version, the M47, was introduced just after the war. This sibling of the WC52 was a bit lower, with a somewhat longer bed, but using the same 230cid engine and drivetrain. In the nuclear-powered mind-set of the time, however, this proven little vehicle was redesigned around an air-cooled flat 6-cylinder opposed engine and a GM Torqmatic transmission. The new model was designated the M53, and appeared in 1949. This air-cooled engine could put out 150 hp when it was running, and that wasn't often enough for the Army.

The Army finally got it right that same year by going back to basics. The improved product was called the M37. The new/old truck went back to the same basic engine, with slight modifications. The latest power plant was the T245a water-cooled 230cid flat-head six-banger from Chrysler (Dodge). The vehicle returned to drum brakes and a manual shift (4-speed and 2-speed) transfer case.

The Dodge M37 was designed to offer better off-road performance, easier maintenance, narrower width, and lower height. It went into production in January 1951 and was produced through August 1954. A total of 63,191 were built.

Canada also used the M37, but theirs was powered by the Chrysler 250.6 engine. A total of 4,524 vehicles were produced between October 1951 and December 1955. In June 1957, production began on the M37B1 model.

The B1 offered a better wiring harness and connectors, improved brake system, and revised canvas top. There was one drawback: a different type of steel was used in the body parts, which made the M37B1 more prone to rust. A total of 47,640 vehicles were produced between April 1958 and June 1968. The total production of all models of the M37 was 115,355 vehicles.

The whole package is tough, strong, and reliable, a truck that can go places and do things. Put the transmission in low, the transfer case in low range, and you can climb a 65 percent grade, even with a full payload, or wade across a stream 42 inches (1m) deep–very slowly, but always moving forward. Simple wooden bench seats can be folded down in the back for transporting six or eight troops, or folded up to carry a generator or fifty cases of C-rations. While the Army tried a few variations on the basic theme, the M37 soldiered on, pretty much as a plain vanilla light-utility truck, without radios, without GPS, without a diesel engine, and without the many bells and whistles found on modern support vehicles like the HMMWV. A handful were converted to wreckers, others to mobile repair trucks (V41). A very few were built up as M42 command trucks, and a lot into the M43 ambulance. All used a 24-gallon (90.8L) fuel tank, a 24-volt electrical system, 9X16 tires, and a bed space that was 78 inches (1.9m) long by 64 inches (1.6m) wide.

Most came equipped with a fire extinguisher and a full set of "pioneer" tools, including a shovel to dig yourself out of the muck. An axe and a pick were mounted on a rack on the M-37's tailgate. There was also a 5-gallon (18.9L) gas can, canvas bed cover, and canvas cab enclosure.

About 100,000 M37s, M37B1s, and M42s were built between 1950 and 1968. Many are still around and in service with Third World nations. They are popular today with military vehicle collectors who pick them up for anywhere from about $300, for a parts vehicle, to around $10,000. Occasionally, sellers try to get a lot more. One was recently advertised in the Robb Report for $25,000.

COLLECTING MILITARY VEHICLES

Collecting military vehicles has become an extremely popular activity, and sometimes in the most unexpected places. In Finland, for example, the Military Vehicle Restoration Club is the largest organization dedicated to any kind of automotive collecting in the country. Americans might be surprised to know that huge numbers of jeeps are alive and well and driving on the wrong side of the road in England, Scotland, Australia, and South Africa—and going to shows where all kinds of ex-military vehicles stand at attention in glittering rows. There are many preserved and restored old war horses running around Denmark, Sweden, and Norway, too—plus others in France, Belgium, and the Netherlands.

HEY, BUDDY—WANNA BUY A TANK?

You, yes you, can buy a tank—and sometimes for very little money. Greg Taylor, who restored some of the tanks and other vehicles shown in this book, bought a couple of Russian T-55s a few years ago for about $3,000 each. He runs them around in the desert outside his Nevada home, and sometimes rents them out for motion picture productions.

Jacques Littlefield, some of whose extensive collection is also shown here, owns one of the two T-72s in American private hands, plus many other tanks and combat vehicles, complete with their weapons. Restored and running Shermans currently sell for more than $50,000. M6 Greyhound armored cars go for about $25,000, depending on condition. WarPac tanks and vehicles sell for a bit less. British Chieftains were going

BELOW: Alan Cors owns this early M3 Stuart, part of his very large collection. OPPOSITE: Joe Cardoza pops up from the engine compartment of his World War II Bren carrier. His house has a two-tank garage, which also contains a late-model and nearly perfect FV 101 Scorpion.

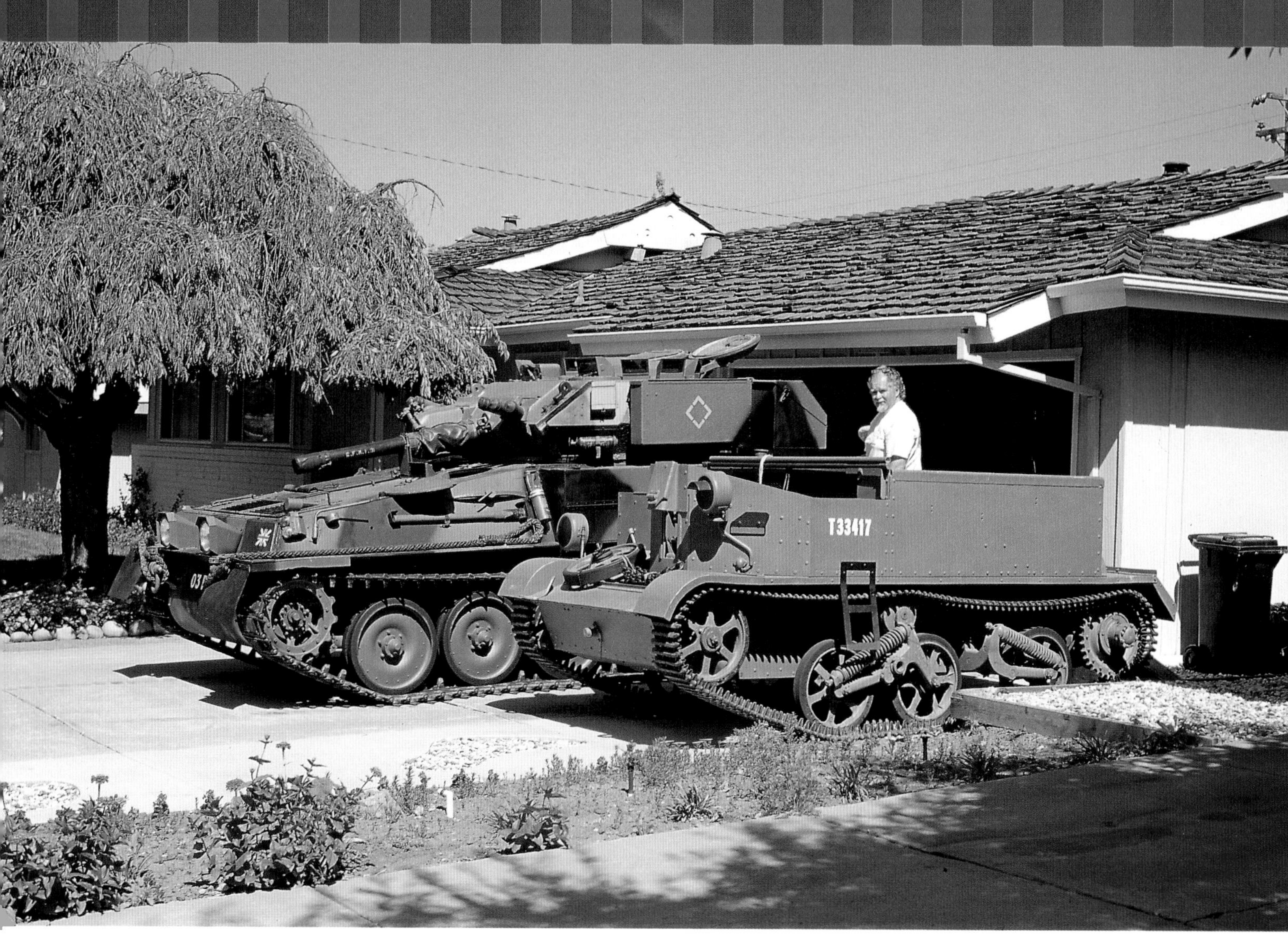

for a paltry £8,000 (about $14,000) fairly recently. That's the approximate value of scrap iron.

Tanks are available from just a few dealers, notably Budge in the U.K. The shipping charges from England to anywhere else in the world are likely to be more than the price of a jeep or M37 in pristine condition. Light armor–including WWII half-tracks, Bren carriers, and APCs from ex-WarPac and ex-NATO forces–is less expensive to buy and to ship.

But those are big, exotic vehicles. For smaller garages, a dealer in Arizona posted an ad on one of the Internet discussion groups recently offering U.S. Vietnam War–era Scorpion self-propelled guns for between $3,500 and $5,500. These vehicles were missing their cannon but were otherwise complete.

Most popular are the wheeled vehicles, the ones you can fill up with grandchildren and use on recon missions in search of ice-cream cones and candy. In this category, the GPW and MB jeeps of WWII vintage take the prize. There are thousands of them, with clubs of their own, and even numerous web sites dedicated to keeping them running and in pristine condition. Rough "project" jeeps are available in California for anywhere from a few hundred dollars (for a basketcase with a seized engine) up to around $10,000 for factory-fresh vehicles, with radios and maybe a .30cal machine gun, and ready to show.

"Most collectors tend to specialize in a particular period of vehicle, such as World War II– or Korean War–era models," Kurt Lesser says, and he should know. He's president of the San Jose, California, chapter of MVPA. "Some guys are interested in armor and, if they can't afford a tank, might buy a half-track or armored personnel carrier.

"The average jeep sells for between $500 and $2,000, after which the owner will invest many hours and hundreds or thousands of additional dollars in new parts and additional pieces to bring the vehicle up to the owner's standards. If you just want to use the vehicle as something fun to drive, that will mean a few hundred dollars for new tires, battery,

LEFT: Another one of Alan Cors' vehicles, this M16 half-track with quad-.50cal machine guns is displayed to the public annually and sometimes used in motion pictures and television productions.

paint, and maybe canvas. That's one kind of restoration. Another is the desire to have something precisely accurate down to the last nut and bolt. If you're planning to show a WWII Ford jeep, you need to be sure that every piece of hardware has the proper 'F' stamped in the head, or you'll lose points during judging."

Another extremely popular vehicle with collectors in the United States is the sturdy ¾-ton (681kg) Dodge pickup truck called the M37 or M38. These things are tremendously durable, tough as nails, and can absorb a whole platoon of neighborhood kids. The power steering on an M37 is provided only by the driver's arms–and you need to have arms like Arnold Schwarzenegger–but that's part of the whole experience. The M37 has standard GI air conditioning, too–i.e., you can take the top down, if you wish, and fold the windshield flat to stay cool. The top local price for an absolutely perfect M37–with radios, pioneer tools, and manuals, and in mint condition–is only $6,500, and there are always a few available to choose from.

PARTS IS PARTS

You'd think, too, that parts for these old vehicles would be hard to find, but so many were made, and then sold to the public, that virtually any part for those ancient little Jeeps is readily available, and from numerous sources. There are still warehouses full of original parts, still in their crates and wrappings, available for sale as "new-old stock" (NOS to the collectors) by mail order or at shows.

A WWII jeep engine, complete with all accessories, perfectly preserved and in its crate, recently materialized and caused a small sensation within the jeep collector/restoration community. It will be preserved in somebody's collection of cool jeep stuff rather than installed, because rebuilt jeep engines are still easy to find.

RIGHT: This M3 Grant, a veteran of the British Army in North Africa, was rescued by Alan Cors and restored to its old splendor.

Radios for vehicles had been readily available until recently. The U.S. government has started destroying rather than selling tactical radios. This is a bit of fallout from the Gulf War when surplus communication gear was discovered in Iraqi vehicles.

"There isn't a part for the MB or GPW jeeps that isn't available today,

either as new-old stock, or reproduction," says Littlefield. "And the M37s were made by the thousands and used around the world. There are still warehouses of original parts available for them."

Also available are the really hard-to-find things like vehicle data plates, new wiring harness and kits, gaskets, tracks for half-tracked and fully tracked armor, and even uniform items to wear while driving your historic vehicle in parades and displays.

LOADED FOR BEAR

Part of the appeal of military vehicles is their association with military operations, and even the most modest of jeeps once mounted heavy firepower. Very few collectors today can get ATF (the Alcohol, Tobacco, and Firearms Division of the U.S. Department of Justice) approval for firing machine guns or weapons of large caliber. Some states, of course, are more liberal than others about the ownership and operation of machine guns. In fact, it isn't impossible to own a firing

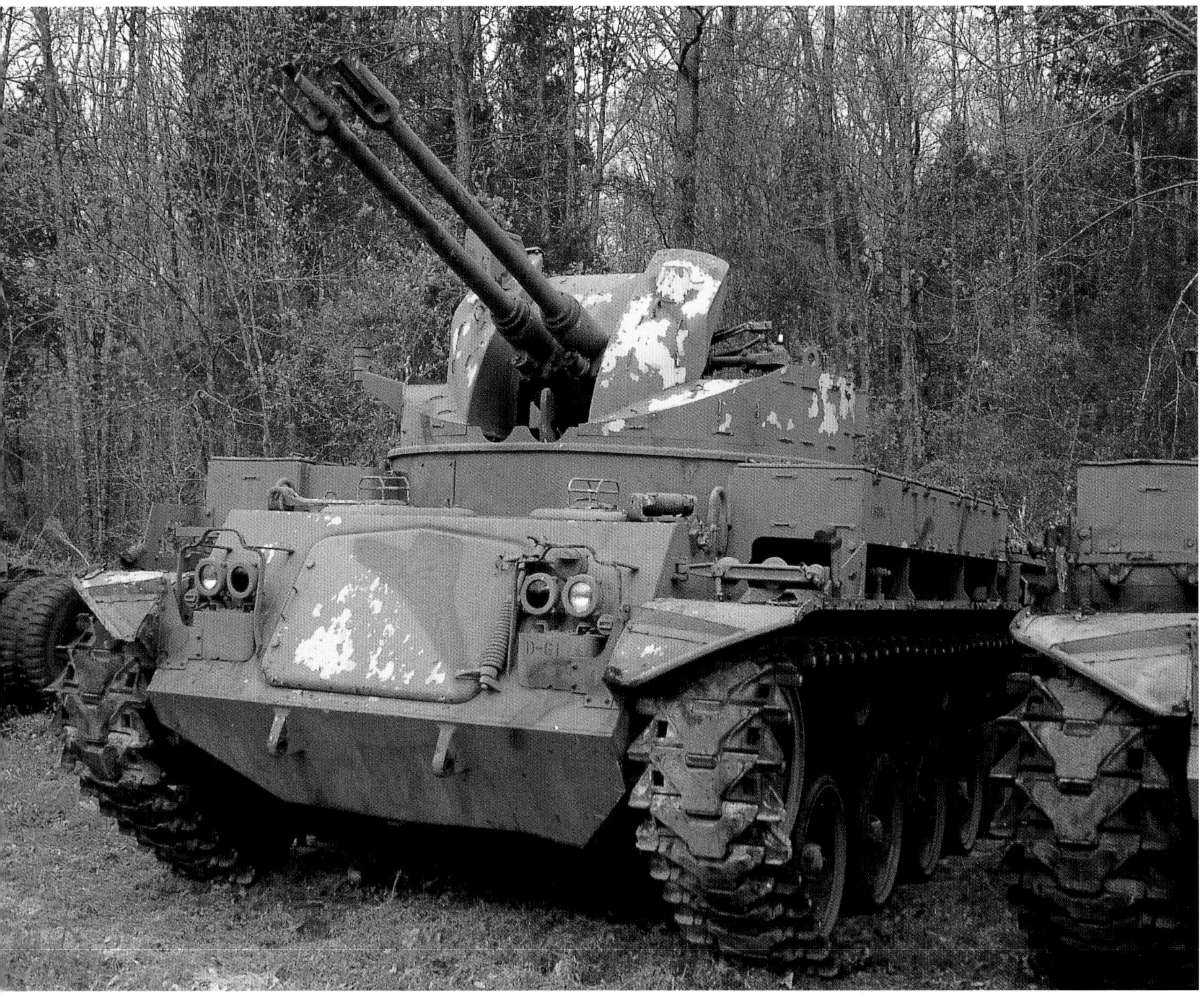

automatic weapon, an anti-tank gun, or even a howitzer.

But American law permits display of nonfiring replicas, or real weapons that have been "de-milled"–and that's the kind you'll usually find on collector vehicles. Generally, these weapons are de-milled, or deactivated, by cutting away parts of the breechblock or by cutting a hole in the side of the barrel. Machine guns are also readily available–made out of wood, from one supplier, or with solid cast breech assemblies from another. Half a dozen American manufacturers supply these display weapons, usually assembled from de-milled components.

Parts kits for .50cal and .30cal machine guns can be easily had for a few hundred dollars. These kits allow you to assemble what looks like a functional weapon from mostly original parts–but they are incapable of firing, or of ever being made to fire real ammunition.

"Gun rings, pintle assemblies, almost every kind of mount, and many kinds of display weapons are available for sale at the conventions," Lesser says. "The hardest part is coming up with the right gun for your particular vehicle–a 1944 mount and ammunition cradle for a .50cal M2 machine gun, for example. That's when you really need to get fussy about what you're going to buy."

Also available are all the manuals for these vehicles, including the highly detailed Field Manuals (FMs) and Technical Manuals (TMs) used for maintenance and overhaul. These manuals include detailed parts lists, exploded drawings, and step-by-step procedures for working on every part of the vehicle. Original FMs and TMs

OPPOSITE: Even M42 "Dusters" with twin 40mm cannons are up for grabs, for about the price of a used car–less than $10,000. You can't drive it down to the bank or the store, but some people own them to take to shows. The cannons have been cut but everything else is functional.

often sell for around $10 each at shows. Reproductions are also available for many of the more popular vehicles.

SUPPORT GROUPS AND THE INTERNET

Jeep fanatics can get into impassioned debates about restoration issues in Internet chat rooms. These arguments can make for entertaining reading. Recently, two factions have been battling over the issue of using reproduction body panels, available and inexpensive, instead of repairing original body panels that have been damaged by rust or abuse. The opposing sides have been lobbing reproduction grenades at each other, and trying to fire their de-milled .50cal pintle-mounted machine guns at each other.

A more common thread of discussion involves problems with vehicles and their diagnosis and repair. If your jeep starts running rough, and you've tried all the obvious fixes without success, a call for help on the Net will bring a flood of expert (and sometimes misguided amateur) advice–at no cost or obligation.

Mostly, though, military vehicle collectors are a friendly, generous bunch. Several major collector organizations provide information and support. The biggest of these are the Military Vehicle Trust (MVT) in England and the Military Vehicle Preservation Association (MVPA) in the United States.

Many generous people publish very interesting and useful information on the Internet. It is like having a big reference book available for free. George Bradford's AFV site, based around his magazine of the same title, is loaded with facts and photos. Numerous sites feature jeeps, and many promote M37 ownership and history. Most include links to other sites with a related focus.

PERIODICALS FOR MV HISTORIANS AND COLLECTORS

Several excellent magazines published in the United States, Canada, England, and Europe are devoted to the interests of military vehicle collectors.

One of the best is David Ahl's *Military Vehicles* magazine, published six times a year. It's loaded with ads for complete vehicles and components. *Military Vehicles* generally includes detailed articles on the history of individual models, plus reports on rallies, advice on restoration, historic photos, and lots of classified ads. (For information, write to *Military Vehicles*, 12 Indian Head Road, Morristown, NJ 07960 USA; send e-mail to mvehicle @aol.com; or visit their website at http://members.aol.com/mvehicle/home.htm.)

Another great resource is *Supply Line*, the publication of the MVPA. *Supply Line* includes lots of ads for all kinds of vehicles, plus all the news from MVPA, and that's usually a lot. There are always many ads for radio gear, wiring harness, data plates, and spare parts for just about any wheeled vehicle from the U.S. inventory since World War II.

For all of those M37 fanatics, *Power Wagon Advertiser* is the periodical of choice, dedicated only to the M37 and its close kin. The address is 3090 Benton Iowa Road, Norway, Iowa 52318-9510 USA. As of February 1997, subscription rates are USA $34.00, Canada and Mexico $46.00. In all other countries the rate is $64.00.

George R. Bradford publishes a wonderful little magazine called *AFV News*. It's a fascinating periodical stuffed to the gills with highly detailed and historically accurate information for armor aficionados worldwide. The AFV Association was formed in 1964 to support the thoughts and research of all those interested in Armored Fighting Vehicles and related topics. To this end, *AFV News* magazine came to be in 1965, and has been published regularly since.

LEFT: **Old military Land Rovers are often very cheap, parts are readily available, and you can drive them on the highway without getting arrested. But they can be pretty ragged when sold by the government.**

AFV News has always featured high-quality photo halftones, the majority of which have never been published elsewhere. Submissions of both armor photos and articles by the membership have been steady over the years. Many authors are revered armor researchers: William Auerbach, Barry Beldam, Charles Bogart, Peter Brown, Mike Cecil, Peter Cooke, Bruce Culver, Don Dingwall, Hilary Doyle, Phil Dyer, Bob Fleming, Michael Green, Richard Harley, Paul Handel, Hal Hock, Robert J. Icks, Thomas Jentz, Chris Johnson, Akira Kikuchi, Charles Kliment, Miles Krogfus, Janusz Magnuski, Jim Mesko, Bill Murphy, Nicola Pignato, Jeff Plowman, Cookie Sewell, Hanno Spoelstra, Raymond Surlemont, Pierre Touzin, Geoff Walden, B.T. White, Steven Zaloga, etc.

For more information about this publication, write *AFV News*, c/o George Bradford, RR 32, Cambridge, Ontario, Canada N3H 4R7.

Wheels & Tracks is an excellent British magazine devoted to military vehicle collecting and preservation. For information, contact Battle of Britain Prints International Ltd., Church House, Church Street, London E15 3JA UK. U.S. subscriptions are handled by RZM Imports, P.O. Box 995, Southbury, CT 06488 USA, (203) 264-0774.

ORGANIZATIONS

THE MILITARY VEHICLE TRUST

The Military Vehicle Trust is one of the largest specialist organizations for the military vehicle enthusiast, with members worldwide. Originally formed as the Military Vehicle Conservation Group in 1968, its aim is to help fellow enthusiasts stay in contact with one another, and to provide all kinds of backup for its members and member groups (Areas).

You do not have to have a vehicle to be a member. Just an interest in the hobby is enough. The Area groups are the main means of supporting the members. It is at their local meetings that many events are organized and the news is spread. While there, valuable help and information can be gained from other vehicle owners.

On a much wider scale, the Trust's committee represents the membership at all levels–from governmental departments to individuals seeking verification of their own vehicle. The Trust provides a quarterly magazine, *Windscreen*, with articles that look at every aspect of vehicle ownership and other related subjects. There is also a bimonthly newsletter, which helps to keep the membership abreast of events of interest that are coming up. There are also the vital sales ads, along with requests for that elusive part needed to finish off a restoration.

Throughout the years, wherever possible, the Trust has taken an active part in supporting ex-servicemen's charities by providing vehicles for fund-raising events or parades. The Trust also helps TV and film companies by finding vehicles for motoring programs, period dramas, and cinematic films.

The Trust helps the military vehicle enthusiast pursue his hobby. If you would like to join, write to them at The Military Vehicle Trust, P.O. Box 6, Fleet, Hampshire, GU13 9PE, England, or send e-mail to their chairman at johnsmith@mvt.org.uk.

MILITARY VEHICLE PRESERVATION ASSOCIATION (MVPA)

MVPA has about eight thousand members worldwide. Most are in the United States, and about 90 percent own at least one ex-military vehicle. The organization was formed in 1976 to support people collecting and restoring all kinds of military vehicles from all nations. It has grown into a large, vibrant organization with about forty chapters in the United States and fifteen abroad.

The affiliated local MVPA chapters hold regular, sometimes large, rallies and shows. Dozens or hundreds of vehicles show up for these events. Vendors of parts and paraphernalia show up, too.

There is an annual national convention at various cities around the U.S. The 1997 convention had more than 150 vendors and two hundred vehicles, with several thousand people in attendance.

MVPA publishes two magazines, *Supply Line* and *Army Motors*, both of which are a benefit of membership. *Supply Line* is a one-hundred-page magazine that comes out six times a year–a place for members to buy, sell, and trade vehicles, parts, supplies, and accessories, with a list of upcoming events and MVPA club news.

Army Motors covers historic and technical issues and is published quarterly. Along with a lot of color, it includes a Tech Talk section, where readers can write in for help with restoration problems, and Sergeant Safety, a column dealing with safety issues. The group also maintains an excellent Internet site and a book club.

Dues are $30 for U.S. residents, $43 for overseas. For information, write to Military Vehicle Preservation Association, P.O. Box 520378, Independence, MO, 64052-0378 USA. Tel: 816-737-5111; Fax: 816-737-5423. E-mail: mvpa-hq@ mvpa.org, or visit their web site at http://www. mvpa.org/.

MIL-VEH MAILING LIST AND ARCHIVES ONLINE

A dedicated Military Vehicle Internet Mailing List, the MIL-VEH List, is accessible online. It is fully automated. Messages are sent to a central point and remailed to list subscribers. It has carried messages as diverse as a DUKW-parts-wanted note, reports of MV activities in Australia, and an account of the shutdown of a military vehicle museum in Riga, Latvia, with military vehicles going at bargain-basement prices. To subscribe to the MIL-VEH List, go to the online subscription application at http: //skylee.com/mil-veh.html. Archived messages from the MIL-VEH List are also available online. To access the archived messages from the MIL-VEH List, go to http://skylee.com/ archives/mil-veh/index.html.

TANK MUSEUMS

THE TANK MUSEUM

Without doubt, the best current display of armor accessible to the public is the Tank Museum at Bovington, Dorset, in the south of England, near the town of Wool. Not only does this institution have a huge fleet of beautifully restored tanks and armor, nicely housed, from the earliest days of World War I; they frequently fire up some of the best of these vehicles and run them around to the amazement of visitors. The best displays, however, come on the annual Battle Day, held on the last Sunday in July, when reenactors and tanks re-create battles and skirmishes from armor history. These displays have, in recent years, included the museum's treasured Mark IV "Male" tank, a veteran of the Battle of Amiens in August 1918, and, more recently, a perfectly restored PzKpfw III in excellent running condition.

These tanks, and their accompanying infantry, duke it out with hordes from the loyal opposing team, firing blanks and making a tremendous amount of smoke and noise.

Bovington's displays are extensive and inclusive, with just about everything imaginable, both historic and contemporary. Tours and rides in armored vehicles are offered. The place is so popular it has its own restaurant–but is not so authentic that you can lunch on bully beef, canned peaches, sand flies, and tea, as did the fabled Desert Rats for three meals a day, for weeks on end.

Many of Bovington's tanks can be driven. There is a large training area within the complex (known as Gallows Hill) where you might see ancient Matildas and Shermans rumbling around in the dirt. It is a busy, popular place with an active research program, a battalion of volunteers, and a lot to offer anyone interested in armor. Highly recommended, and worth the trip, even for Americans. Write to the Tank Museum, Bovington, Dorset, BH20 6JG, England, Or call 01929 096.

OTHER TANK MUSEUMS AND ARMOR DISPLAYS

- A.A.F. Tank Museum, Mattituck, NY, USA
- Aberdeen Proving Ground, Ordnance Museum, Aberdeen, MD, USA
- Armored Vehicle Maint. Centre, Segovia, Spain
- Artillery Academy, Segovia, Spain
- Auto Und Technik Museum, Sinsheim, Germany
- Bovington Tank Museum, Wareham, Dorset, England
- Brussels Tank Museum, Brussels, Belgium
- BWB War Museum, Koblenz, Germany
- Camp Blanding, Starke, FL, USA
- Camp Mabry, Texas Military History Museum, Austin, TX, USA (Hetzer, M4)
- Canadian Artillery Museum, Cfb Shilo, Manitoba, Canada
- El Goloso Barracks, Madrid, Spain
- First Division Museum, Wheaton, IL, USA
- Ft. Bragg, 82nd Airborne Museum, Fayetteville, NC, USA
- Ft. Benning, US Army Infantry Museum, Columbus, GA, USA
- Ft. Benning Museum, Columbus, GA, USA
- Ft. Hood, 1st Cav. Div. and 2nd Arm. Div. Museums, TX, USA
- Ft. Knox, Patton Museum, KY, USA
- Ft. Lee, Quartermasters Museum, Petersburg, VA, USA
- Ft. Meade, Maryland, near Washington, D.C., USA
- Ft. Stewart, Hinesville, Georgia, USA (Iraqi Armor)
- Hackenberg War Museum, Veckring, France
- Haerens Kampskole, Oksboel, Denmark
- Imperial War Museum, Duxford, Cambridgeshire, England
- Israeli Army Armor School, Latrun, Israel
- Kubinka Tank Museum, Niibt Collection, near Moscow, Russia
- Leningrad Artillery Museum, Leningrad, Russia
- Lenin Prospeki Memorial, Sarny, Ukraine
- Military Museum, Belgrade, Serbia
- Military Museum, Kbely, Prague, Czechoslovakia
- Military Museum, Sofia, Bulgaria
- Military Museum, Oslo, Norway
- Military Museum of Southern New England, Danbury, CT, USA
- Motor Technik Museum, Bad Oeynhausen, Germany
- Museo Militar, Bucharest, Romania
- Museum of Military History, Indianapolis, IN, USA
- Mussee Memorial, Bayeux, France
- Navy Yard and Marine Museum, Washington, D.C., USA
- Pansarmuseet, Axvall, Sweden
- Panssarimuseo, Parola, Finland
- Panzermuseum, Munster, Germany
- Panzermuseum, Thun, Switzerland
- Petawawa, Cfb Petawawa, Ontario, Canada
- Quantico Air/Ground Museum, VA, USA
- RAAC Tank Museum, Puckapunyal, Victoria, Australia
- Rock Island Arsenal, IL, USA
- Saumur Armour Museum, Anjou, France
- Shilo Artillery Museum, Cfb Shilo, Manitoba, Canada
- Tank Collection: E.R.G.M.E.B., Gien, France
- Tojhmuseet, Copenhagen, Denmark
- Vermont Vets Militia Museum, Colchester, VT, USA
- Victory Memorial Museum, Hondelange, Belgium
- Vimy House, Canadian War Museum, Ottawa, Canada
- War Memorial, Volokolamsk, Russia
- War Museum Collection, Trieste, Italy
- Worthington Tank Museum, Cfb Borden, Ontario, Canada
- WWII and Korean LTV Museum, Camp Pendleton, CA, USA

MILITARY VEHICLE CLUBS

Belgium Military Vehicle Trust
Rudiger AE Geudens,
Laarstraat 16 9170 St-Gillis-Waas
Belgium
Tel: +32.(0)3/707.13.48
bn000050@belgonet.bn

Blue and Gray Military Vehicle Trust
District of Columbia, USA
301-867-4944

M.V.C.C. Paris
ILE DE FRANCE
33 1 3054 3091

Ex-Military Land Rover Association
Mark Cook
50 St. Andrew Street
Leighton Buzzard,
Beds. LU7 8DS
01525 372016

M.V.C.C. Glendale, Calif.
SCMVCC, 9260
Campo Road,
Spring Valley, CA 91977 USA

WILLYS CLUB
795 N. Evans St.
Pottstown, PA 19464 USA
610-326-2907
gowillys@ix.netcom.com

OTHER RESOURCES

NORWAY

It may come as a surprise to Americans that military vehicle collection and restoration is very popular in Norway. WWII vintage vehicles stayed in service with that nation's armed forces until quite recently and–when no longer needed–were sold to civilian buyers. A very active collector organization, Historiske Militaere Kjoretoyers Forening, provides support for members, as well as anyone else interested in Norwegian military vehicles. For information, contact David Hammond, Historiske Militaere Kjoretoyers Forening–Norway, Postboks 51 Blindern, 0313 Oslo Norway. Ph off +47 22 33 42 60, E-mail davidh@oslonett.no

MANUALS FOR MILITARY VEHICLES

Copies of the required manuals for virtually all collectible U.S. vehicles are available, in reprint form, from Portrayal Press, P.O. Box 1190, Andover, NJ 07821 USA.

DATA AND SPECIFICATIONS FOR WWII ARMOR

Very detailed and complete data sheets for all kinds of vehicles and weapons used during World War II are available on disk from CINC Software Co., P.O. Box 34531, Richmond, VA 23234-0531. These spec sheets are extremely detailed and of great interest to the modeler or student of arms and armor. The current cost is about $40, including postage, but write for current charges.

M37 PARTS

As an example of the wealth of resources for anyone contemplating a restoration project, here is a partial list of U.S. companies specializing in parts for the Dodge M37:

- A.B. Linn, Salisbury, NC 704-637-9076
- Adirondack Dodge Parts and Surplus, Prospect, NY 800-932-8020
- CAMO Inc, Stroudsburg, PA 717-476-8333
- Jack's Government Surplus, Tuscon, AZ 520-574-0300
- MARS, Nashville, IN 812-988-2330
- Sarafan, Spring Valley, NY 914-356-1080
- Sultan Dodge, Phoenix, OR 541-535-3522
- Vermont Commercial Salvage, Colchester, VT 802-864-4762
- Veteran Vehicles, Wrentham, MA 508-384-7698
- Vintage Power Wagons, Fairfield, IA 515-472-4665

INDEX

PHOTO CREDITS

©John Blackman: pp. 134-135

E.W. Fowler Collection: Endpapers; pp. 9, 11, 12-13, 19 top, 19 bottom, 38 center left, 41 top right, 46, 48-49, 62-63, 68 top left, 68-69, 69 bottom right, 71 top, 74 bottom left, 76, 77, 78-79, 100 bottom left, 100-101, 102-103, 113 , 125, 126-127, 128, 130 bottom left, 137 bottom right, 138 top left, 138-139, 140-141, 143, 144-145, 149, 150, 152 top, 152 bottom, 156-157, 162-163, 164, 165, 167, 170-171, 172-173, 177 top right

Michael Green Collection: pp. 17, 26, 31, 34, 36, 39, 40-41, 41 bottom left, 42 top, 42 bottom, 43, 44 top left, 44-45, 55 bottom, 56 top, 57, 66 top, 66-67, 71 bottom, 72-73, 74-75, 119, 131, 134, 142, 158, 160, 182, 183, 184, 186

©Hans Halberstadt: pp. 2, 6, 8, 15, 20, 21, 22 bottom left, 24 bottom left, 24-25, 28, 29, 30, 32, 33, 47, 48 bottom left, 50, 51 top, 51 bottom, 52-53, 56 top, 56 bottom, 58-59 top, 59 top right, 80 bottom left, 80-81, 82-83, 83 top right, 83 bottom left, 84, 85, 86, 87, 88 top left, 88-89, 90 top, 90 bottom, 92-93, 104bottom left, 104-105, 106, 107 bottom, 108-109, 111, 112, 114 center left, 114-115, 116 top left, 116-117, 118 top, 118 bottom, 119, 120 bottom left, , 122-123, 130-131, 134 top left, 137 top left, 142, 147, 150-151, 153, 155, 159, 168, 169, 171 top right, 174-175, 176-177, 180, 181, 187, 189

Hans Halberstadt Collection: pp. 10, 18, 21-22, 44 top, 72-73, 94 bottom left,
98, 99, 124

Sam Katz Collection: pp. 94 bottom left, 94-95, 98, 99

National Archives: pp. 26-27, 38-39, 54, 55 top left, 64 bottom left, 67, 72 bottom, 120-121, 132-133

©I.D.F. Spokeman: pp. 96-97

©Greg Stewart: p. 107 top

©The Tank Museum: pp. bottom 42, 66 bottom left

U.S. Army Photograph: pp. 16-17, 44-45, 61, 64-65, 136

U.S. Army Signal Corps: pp. 31, 34